IMAGES OF W

AMERICAN WHEELED ARMOURED FIGHTING VEHICLES

RARE PHOTOGRAPHS FROM WARTIME ARCHIVES

Michael Green

Pen & Sword
MILITARY

First published in Great Britain in 2016 by
PEN & SWORD MILITARY
An imprint of
Pen & Sword Books Ltd
47 Church Street
Barnsley
South Yorkshire
S70 2AS

ISBN 978-1-47385-436-9

Typeset by Concept, Huddersfield, West Yorkshire HD4 5JL.
Printed and bound in India by Replika Press Pvt. Ltd.

Pen & Sword Books Ltd incorporates the imprints of Pen & Sword Archaeology, Atlas, Aviation, Battleground, Discovery, Family History, History, Maritime, Military, Naval, Politics, Railways, Select, Social History, Transport, True Crime, and Claymore Press, Frontline Books, Leo Cooper, Praetorian Press, Remember When, Seaforth Publishing and Wharncliffe.

For a complete list of Pen & Sword titles please contact
PEN & SWORD BOOKS LIMITED
47 Church Street, Barnsley, South Yorkshire S70 2AS, England
E-mail: enquiries@pen-and-sword.co.uk
Website: www.pen-and-sword.co.uk

Contents

Dedication

This book is dedicated to Colonel Royal P. Davidson, an officer in the Illinois National Guard, who was the first to mount a weapon and armour on an American wheeled vehicle in 1898.

Foreword

From the very earliest and crude designs of placing a machine gun on a car with an armoured shield, to the behemoth Mine Resistant Ambush Protected (MRAP) vehicles used in Iraq and Afghanistan. The author takes the reader through the design, testing, development, acceptance and use in the armed forces of the United States of wheeled armoured fighting vehicles from the First World War, up to the conflicts in Iraq and Afghanistan.

It becomes clear – through the author's tracing of the developmental history of systems – that there is a distinct linkage to previous designs and systems; in some cases to improve on failed designs. The HMMWV (High Mobility Multipurpose Wheeled Vehicle) is a great example. Originally designed as a replacement for a number of stop-gap rear area vehicles, in 2003 it quickly found itself conducting convoy security in Iraq, a task it was never designed for. The US Army responded with the Up-Armored HMMWV.

The downside of the Up-Armored HMMWV program was the fact that the vehicle had never been intended to carry that much extra weight, which badly strained its engine power capacity, transmissions and suspension systems. Another consequence of surrounding American troops with armour protection in their Up-Armored HMMWVs was the interior heat build-up, which required air conditioners. Unfortunately, these drained even more power and greatly increased fuel consumption for the vehicle. It got to the point where the Up-Armored HMMWVs were called 'groaners' by those who served on them due to how heavy they had become.

In sharp contrast to its long-time preference for fully-tracked armoured fighting vehicles, the US Army eventually embraced the concept of wheeled armoured fighting vehicles with the introduction of the eight-wheel Stryker in 2002. Combat experience soon resulted in a host of modifications to the vehicle. Unlike the HMMWV, the Stryker was built to expand and incorporate modifications without altering the original design.

As the Stryker changed how the US Army went to war, the MRAP changed how America's wheeled armoured fighting vehicles would be designed in the future, with all being fitted with mine resistant 'V' shaped hulls, and a host of soldier protection features.

Randy R. Talbot
Command Historian (retired)
US Army TACOM Life Cycle Management Command

Acknowledgments

As with any published work, authors must depend on a great many people for assistance. These included over many years my fellow author and long-time mentor the late Richard Hunnicutt and my good friend Brent Sauer, who was kind enough to allow me to use some of his pictures for this work. Other friends who kindly supplied pictures for this work are credited in the captions.

Both the paid and volunteer staff of the now closed Patton Museum of Armor and Cavalry provided me with a great deal of assistance. Former museum volunteers who made an extra effort to assist me include Dean and Nancy Kleffman, as well as Don Moriarty. For the sake of brevity, all images from the former Patton Museum of Cavalry and Armor will be credited to the 'Patton Museum'.

Peter Keating, director of communications for General Dynamics Land Systems (GDLS), was very generous with pictorial support as always. All those from the firm will be shortened to GDLS. Craig McNab, the director of communications for AM General, also contributed images for this book and answered many questions.

Pictures acquired from various Department of Defense (DOD) web sites, which include Defense Imagery.mil, and Defense Video & Imagery Distribution System (DVIDS). For the sake of brevity, all will be credited to the 'DOD'.

A US Army entity that assisted the author in acquiring historical photographs for this work was the Command Historian's Office of the TACOM Life Cycle Management Command (LCMC). All pictures from this organization are credited to 'TACOM', for the sake of brevity.

Notes to the Reader

1. The main focus of this work is the employment of American-designed and built wheeled armoured fighting vehicles (AFVs) in American military service, and not their use in foreign military service.
2. The starting point for the Second World War in this work will not reflect its official beginning in September 1939. Rather, this work will use December 1941, the month of America's official entry into the conflict.
3. For those unfamiliar with 4×4, 6×6, 8×8 or other number combinations mentioned in this work: the first numeral represents the numbers of wheels on a given vehicle, the second numeral identifies the number of driven (powered) wheels on that vehicle.

Chapter One

Pre-Second World War Wheeled AFVs

In 1898, Colonel Royal P. Davidson, an officer in the Illinois National Guard, mounted a machine gun protected by an armoured shield on a small Duryea three-wheeled car. This was America's first wheeled armoured fighting vehicle (AFV), although it never entered into US Army service. He later mounted the same armoured shield protected machine gun on a four-wheel Duryea car.

Davidson went on to progressively develop a series of new armoured cars, based on the chassis of Cadillacs. In 1910, Davidson displayed several partially armoured, machine gun equipped vehicles, and in 1914 he unveiled a fully armoured, machine gun equipped armoured car. Despite Davidson's best efforts, the US Army showed no interest in his vehicles.

Other Contenders

Davidson was not alone in envisioning a future for wheeled AFVs with the American military. In 1915, the US Army tested a vehicle they referred to as 'Armored Car No. 1'. It was a fully armoured machine gun equipped vehicle based on the chassis of the 'Jeffery Quad' truck.

The White Motor Company came up with their own vehicle in 1915, which the US Army labelled 'Armored Car No. 2'. Like the Jeffery vehicle, it was a based on a four-wheeled truck chassis, completely armoured, and armed with machine guns.

In 1916, the New York National Guard acquired three open-topped armoured cars. Each vehicle built upon a different commercial truck chassis. That same year, the US Army pressed into service all three of the New York National Guard's new armoured cars, as well as both the Jeffery and White armoured cars, for use during the Mexican Expedition, which lasted from 1916 to 1917.

The Marines Get Involved

The US Marine Corps (USMC) acquired a single King Armored Car from the Armored Motor Car Company in 1916, with two more acquired the following year. The King Armored Cars were fully armoured, and armed with a single turret-mounted small-calibre machine gun. They were based on the chassis of a 4 × 2 car designed and built by the King Motor Car Company.

The USMC testing of the three King Armored Cars went well enough that eight more were ordered in 1918, which allowed the forming of the 1st Armored Car Squadron. However, not everybody thought the King Armored Car was worth acquiring. In a 1919 report by a USMC captain named Drum appears this extract:

> Found only seven in commission and five of these put through testing. Performance not all that good, as the design is poor and insufficient persons available to keep cars in running order. Only well-trained drivers can operate the cars. The XO [executive officer] of the Armored Car squadron, 2Lt Charles B. Long, is one and can handle it in any terrain reasonably expected. Cars are underpowered, weak transmissions, but could render good service if over-hauled. Recommend that of the eight cars at Phil [Philadelphia] six be entirely taken into overhaul, other two have armour removed, use chassis for spares.

Other than taking part in a number of public demonstrations, none of the King Armored Cars would ever see combat. The 1st Armored Car Squadron would be disbanded in 1921, and their vehicles placed into storage. Five King Armored Cars were later pulled out of storage and employed briefly by the USMC during its occupation of Haiti (1915–34). They were returned to storage in 1927 and most were eventually scrapped in 1934. At least two examples of an improved model would be tested by the US Army in the 1920s, with no orders resulting.

The First World War

Before the various combatants had settled into the trench warfare that has come to define the First World War, the British, French, and Belgians had employed improvised armoured cars, based on commercial vehicles, for reconnaissance duties, as well as other roles such as raiding enemy lines and airfield defence.

Despite America's official entry into the First World War in 1917, there were no calls by the US Army for armoured cars at that time. Those in charge felt that the trench fighting being conducted in France did not lend itself to their employment. The USMC had offered to deploy an infantry division to France, along with the 1st Armored Car Squadron, but this offer was rejected by the senior US Army General in that theatre of operation.

During the last few months of the First World War, the Service of Supply organization in France, which was overseen by the US Army Quartermaster Corps, requested armoured cars for the protection of the interior line of communications in that country. However, nothing ever came of the request before 'The War to End all Wars' concluded.

Quartermaster Corps Projects

From the mid-1920s up through the early 1930s, the US Army Quartermaster Corps explored the possibility of using off-the-shelf commercial truck components to develop a series of 4 × 4 vehicles. These vehicles were intended for use as cargo trucks or converted into improvised armoured cars if the need arose.

The first improvised Quartermaster Corps armoured car was labelled the T6-4WD. It featured a machine gun armed turret. The code letter designation 'T' stood for test in the US Army nomenclature system, starting post-First World War. The '4WD' in the vehicle's designation code stood for four-wheel drive. After the construction of the T6, the Quartermaster Corps no longer used the 4WD designation.

The single T6-4WD Armored Car was followed by six units of the improvised T7 Armored Car. Because the T7 was powered by a Franklin Automotive Company car engine, it was sometimes referred to as the 'Franklin Armored Car'.

The Quartermaster Corps also looked at the possibility of using the chassis of various 4 × 2 commercial cars as the basis for improvised armoured cars. This resulted in a number of experimental vehicles labelled the T8, T9 and T10. There was also a small 4 × 2 armoured car submitted by American inventor J. Walter Christie, named the M1933 Airborne Combat Car. None of these experimental armoured cars were ordered into series production by the US Army.

Ordnance Department Projects

In a duplication of effort, the US Army Ordnance Department also explored using the chassis of various 4 × 2 commercial cars as the basis for improvised armoured cars. Like those tested by the Quartermaster Corps, those tested by the Ordnance Department were only partially armoured. The first was the T1 Armored Car, followed by the progressively-improved T2 and T3 Armored Cars.

In 1932, the US Army decided that the T3 would no longer be considered an armoured car, but thereafter be known as the T1 Scout Car. The US Army eventually concluded that scout cars, based on 4 × 2 civilian cars, lacked the necessary off-road capabilities and load-carrying capacity, which ended any further development.

M1 Armored Car

The US Army decided in 1931 to go forward with its first ground-up design for an armoured car, that was originally designated as the T4. It was a 6 × 4 vehicle with front wheels being employed only for steering. The T4 was fully armoured and came with a machine gun equipped turret.

The US Army concluded that the testing process with the T4 went well and, in 1934, standardized the vehicle as the M1 Armored Car, with twenty units ordered. Due to the small number ordered the government-owned and government-operated Rock Island Arsenal was assigned the task of building the vehicles.

Another Armored Car Contender

An unsuccessful rival to the M1 Armored Car was the rear-engine powered T11 Armored Car, which was also fully armoured, and fitted with a machine gun equipped turret. A more capable vehicle than the M1, the 4 × 4 T11 had some unresolved design issues.

Not wanting to give up on the T11 Armored Car, the Ordnance Department awarded the Marmon-Herrington Company a contract to build six improved units, labelled the T11E1, for additional testing. There was also a single revised example of the vehicle, designated the T11E2. None met US Army expectations.

The code letter 'E' in a vehicle's designation meant the original design was modified in some way. The number following the letter 'E' stood for the sequence number of the modification. Hence, you have the T11E1 followed by the T11E2. This designation system also applied to vehicles assigned an M number.

Second-Generation Scout Cars

The first of the new second-generation open-top machine gun armed scout cars was initially designated as the T7 and tested by the US Army in 1934. Upon meeting all the service's expectations, the vehicle was standardized as the M1 Scout Car. Unlike the M1 and T11 Armored Cars, the 4 × 4 M1 Scout Car was an improvised wheeled AFV, based on a commercial chassis frame.

Seventy-six units of the M1 Scout Car were ordered from the designer, the Indiana Motor Corporation, a subsidiary of the White Motor Company. All were delivered between 1934 and 1937.

At the same time, the US Army was testing the T7 Scout Car. They also briefly evaluated a Marmon-Herrington Company Scout Car design. The US Army felt it had some commendable design features that were superior to the White Motor Company offering, but never pursued it. Nor did it bother to assign it an official service designation. There was also a T8, T10 and T11 Scout Car being considered at one point in time, but they never left the drawing board.

Improved Scout Car

On the heels of the acceptance of the M1 Scout Car, the US Army could see the value of adding some design improvements. This resulted in the testing in 1935 of another very similar-looking open-top, machine gun armed vehicle, labelled the T9 Scout Car. The US Army liked what it saw with the 4 × 4 T9 Scout Car and standardized it in 1938 as the M2 Scout Car. The US Army took into its inventory a total of twenty units of the M2 Scout Car in 1938. There were also two upgraded examples of the vehicle built for test purposes, designated the M2E1, which did not enter into production.

The Final Scout Car

Continuous design upgrades to the M2 Scout Car led to an improved model being built that was originally designated M2A1 Scout Car. This was later changed to the M3 Scout Car. The US Army assigned the production of the vehicle to the White Motor Company.

The letter 'A' added to a vehicle's designation code meant it underwent a minor design modification, with the number following the letter 'A' denoting its sequence of production. A major design modification would typically be reflected in the vehicle's designation code by the application of a higher number. This is reflected in the M2A1 Scout Car eventually being relabelled as the M3 Scout Car.

In 1940, White began production of a redesigned model of the M3 Scout Car, which was assigned the designation M3A1 Scout Car. Between 1939 and 1944, the firm would construct 20,894 units of the M3A1 Scout Car. Like the M2, M2A1 and M3, the Diebold Lock & Safe Company provided the armoured bodies for the M3A1 Scout Car.

The USMC ordered hundreds of M3A1 Scout Cars in early 1942. However, once the Corps' attention turned to the difficulties of invading enemy-occupied islands in the Pacific, it was decided that the much smaller and lighter four-wheel drive 0.25-ton truck, better known as the 'Jeep', would be a better choice and the order for the M3A1s was cancelled.

During combat against Axis Forces in the US Army's North African Campaign (November 1942 until May 1943), the M3A1 Scout Car was assigned to US Army armoured reconnaissance battalions. Its lacklustre off-road performance and lack of overhead armour protection made it unpopular, and it was quickly replaced when something better came along.

A reflection of the US Army's lack of confidence in the M3A1 Scout Car can be deduced by the 11,401 units of the vehicle allocated to Lend-Lease, which was in effect from March 1941 until the end of the Second World War. Of that number, 6,987 went to the British Army, 3,310 to the Red Army and 104 to the Nationalist Chinese Army.

Odds and Ends

In 1941, prior to America's official entry into the Second World War, the Smart Engineering Company presented the US Army with a 4 × 4 armoured jeep for consideration, which the service designated as the T25 Scout Car. Despite numerous variants of the T25 series being developed and tested, it was a failure due to the adverse handling characteristics imposed on the vehicle by the addition of armour and weapons it was never designed to carry.

Another armoured scout car submitted to the US Army for consideration in 1941 was an open-top 4 × 4 vehicle designed and built by the Ford Motor Company. It was assigned the strange designation Observation Post Vehicle T2. It was never ordered into production.

The Eight-Wheel Wonder

A pre-Pearl Harbor armoured car submitted to the US Army for consideration was a large eight-wheel 8 × 8 vehicle. It was fully armoured, and had a small open-top weaponless turret. It was designed and built by the Trackless Tank Corporation.

Initially impressed by the off-road capabilities of the Trackless Tank Corporation's product, the US Army anticipated ordering it in several different versions for more intense testing. These would include a T13 Armored Car armed with a 37mm cannon, another armed with a 3-inch gun designated the T7 Tank Destroyer and a third mounting a 105mm howitzer to be referred to as the T39 Self-Propelled Howitzer.

Because the Trackless Tank Corporation lacked the industrial infrastructure to build the large numbers of vehicles the US Army was envisioning, the service demanded that it contract with a much larger firm, in this case Reo Motors, which had the capability to build a large number of vehicles if a contract was awarded.

Due to a series of unforeseen delays, the first two modified examples of the T13 Armored Car built by Reo Motors were not ready for testing by the US Army until the summer of 1942. Upon further testing, a number of serious design flaws cropped up and the entire programme was soon cancelled.

Stranger Than Fiction

The National Defense Research Committee, which was in existence between 1940 and 1941, also attempted to develop a suitable series of wheeled armoured fighting vehicles for US Army consideration. They envisioned a 4 × 4 or 8 × 8 AFV equipped with a hydraulically-operated jumping apparatus. It was intended that the jumping apparatus would allow it to leap over intervening obstacles when moving at high speed. This particular vehicle concept never went past the model stage.

At the very end of the nineteenth century, Colonel Royal P. Davidson of the Illinois National Guard demonstrated a modified three-wheel commercial car fitted with an armoured shield-protected small-calibre machine gun. Shortly thereafter, he modified the same vehicle to have four wheels as seen here. Colonel Davidson is at the controls of the vehicle. (*Patton Museum*)

(*Above*) Colonel Davidson continued to experiment with the development of wheeled armoured fighting vehicles (AFVs) prior to America becoming a participant in the First World War. Pictured is one of his later prototypes, now fully armoured, and based on the chassis of a Cadillac. The driver is protected by a small overhead armoured housing. (*Patton Museum*)

(*Opposite above*) Other individuals and companies were also experimenting with the concept of fully armoured wheeled AFVs. Shown is a rear view of a single prototype vehicle built by the Jeffrey Motor Company the US Army labelled Armored Car No. 1. A novel design feature that appeared with this vehicle was having a driver in both the front and rear of the vehicle. (*Patton Museum*)

(*Opposite below*) Pictured is the White Motor Company prototype vehicle labelled Armored Car No. 2 by the US Army. Like the Jeffery Armored Car No. 1, it was pressed into service by the US Army to patrol the American-Mexican border in 1916 and 1917. Pictured to the left of the armoured car are two motorcycles with sidecars fitted with shield-protected small-calibre machine guns. (*Patton Museum*)

(*Above*) The White Motor Company Armored Car No. 2 rode on large solid rubber wheels as seen here. As with the Jeffery Armored Car No. 1, the vehicle was obviously top-heavy and its off-road ability was no doubt minimal at best as only its rear wheels were driven. It is stated that the vehicle's 36hp engine could propel it to a maximum speed of 40mph on roads. (*Patton Museum*)

(*Opposite above*) In 1916, the New York National Guard was the recipient of three very similar-looking open-topped armoured cars, paid for with private funds. Each of the three armoured cars was built upon a different truck manufacturer's chassis. Pictured is the Mack Brothers' Company version in 1916. It would have been armed with shield-protected small-calibre machine guns. (*Patton Museum*)

(*Opposite below*) Pictured in 1920 is this rear view of the Mack Brother's Company version of the three very similar-looking armoured cars purchased for the New York National Guard in 1916 by private donors. The vehicles weighed approximately 9,000lbs and had a top speed of 30mph. They were 17 feet 8 inches long and 5 feet 5 inches tall. (*Patton Museum*)

A good part of the USMC inventory of King Armored Cars is seen here at a recruiting drive in New York City in 1919. The vehicle had a crew of three, weighted 5,500lbs and was protected by a quarter inch of armour. Power came from a 70hp engine that provided it a maximum speed of 45mph on roads. Visible are the barrels of the small-calibre machine guns they were armed with. (*Patton Museum*)

Post-First World War there appeared a version of the King Armored Car, listed as seen in the picture's caption as the 'King Eight'. There is little information on this version of the vehicle, which bears US Army markings. Unlike earlier armoured car designs that were fitted with solid rubber tyres, the White Armored Car series rode on pneumatic (air-filled) tyres. (*Patton Museum*)

ROCK ISLAND ARSENAL
241-33780 March 1,1920.
King-Eight Armor Car
No.11506 Weight 5540 lb.
Left back.

The Medium Armored Car T2, one of four ordered by the US Army in the late 1920s. All were based on the chassis of the LaSalle luxury car from the General Motors Corporation (GMC). The vehicle was protected by steel armour plate 0.125-inch thick and powered by an 86hp engine that gave it a maximum speed of 70mph. Notice the armoured roof panels in the upright position. *(Patton Museum)*

The US Army never stopped tinkering with the design of its four Medium Armored Car T2s to find the optimum configuration. This resulted in four additional versions of the vehicle series, labelled the T2E1 to T2E4. Pictured is the T2E1 Medium Armored Car. It and the three follow-on models were all fitted with a small one-man open-topped turret fitted with a small-calibre machine gun.
(Patton Museum)

(*Opposite above*) The first American wheeled AFV not based on an existing car or truck chassis was the US Army Armored Car M1 seen here. Unlike the open-topped turrets of previous American wheeled AFVs, the turret of the M1 Armored Car was fully enclosed. It was fitted with a single large-calibre machine gun. There were also two small-calibre machine guns carried in the vehicle. (*Patton Museum*)

(*Opposite below*) The four-man US Army Armored Car M1 weighed over 10,000lbs, with its maximum armour thickness being 0.5-inch. It was powered by a 133hp engine that gave it a top road speed of 55mph. Unlike subsequent American wheeled AFVs, only the rear wheels were driven on the M1 Armored Car. The non-powered front wheels were employed only for steering the vehicle. (*Patton Museum*)

(*Above*) The T7 Armored Car pictured was based on a standard US Army 1.25-ton cargo truck used by the Quartermaster Corps during the interwar period. Like the M1 Armored Car, the T7 had a fully enclosed turret armed with a large-calibre machine gun. In addition, it had two small-calibre machine guns; one mounted to fire out the front of the hull and another out the rear of the hull. (*Patton Museum*)

An unsuccessful competitor to the M1 Armored Car was the T11 Armored Car, which weighed 11,250lbs and was protected by armour up to 0.375-inch thick. Design problems with the T11 uncovered during early testing quickly resulted in it being modified into the T11E1 model show here. Power for the vehicle came from a 115hp engine that gave it a maximum road speed of 70mph. *(Patton Museum)*

The US Army continued to tweak the design of the T11 series Armored Car, which resulted in the single example of the T11E2 Armored Car shown here. Notice the changes to the hull layout and the new turret design. As with other US Army armoured cars of that time, the wheels positioned on either side of the hull were free-spinning and intended to prevent the vehicle from becoming stuck on uneven terrain. *(Patton Museum)*

The open-topped Scout Car T7 constructed in 1934. It was based on the chassis of a 0.5-ton 4 × 4 commercial truck from the White Motor Company. The vehicle weighed 7,700lbs and was powered by a 75hp engine. The maximum armour thickness found on the front of the vehicle was 0.5 inch. Testing went well and it was standardized as the Scout Car M1 in 1934 by the US Army. *(Patton Museum)*

Based on experience gained with the Scout Car M1, the US Army continued with development of the concept, which resulted in the construction of the Scout Car T9. Service tests were successful and the vehicle was standardized as the Scout Car M2, seen here in 1938. It weighed 7,900lbs, and with a 94hp engine had a maximum road speed of 50mph. *(Patton Museum)*

(*Opposite above*) The continuous refinement of the Scout Car M2 led to an improved model designated as the Scout Car M2A1, which was later changed to the Scout Car M3 seen here. It was produced by the White Motor Company and weighed 16,000lbs. Powered by a 95hp engine, it had a top road speed of 60mph. Maximum armour thickness was 0.5-inch on the front of the vehicle. (*Patton Museum*)

(*Opposite below*) Another view of the Scout Car M3 taking part in a pre-Second World War training exercise. The weapon mix on the vehicle consisted of a single unprotected large-calibre machine gun and two shield-protected small-calibre machine guns, as appears in this photograph. Notice the vehicle has a rear door. (*Patton Museum*)

(*Above*) By 1939, a host of design improvements to the Scout Car M3 resulted in a re-designed version being labelled as the M3A1 Scout Car, an example of which is seen here during a pre-Pearl Harbor training exercise within the United States. The front bumper of the M3 Scout Car was replaced with a spring-loaded roller on the M3A1 Scout Car, which is visible in this image. (*Patton Museum*)

(*Opposite above*) One of the key external differences between the M3 and M3A1 Scout Cars was the widening of the body of the latter over the fender wells, as seen in this photograph of a restored example. The M3A1 Scout Car was 18 feet 5 inches in length and had a width of 6 feet 8 inches. It was 6 feet 6.5 inches tall and combat loaded weighed 12,400lbs. (*Pierre-Olivier Buan*)

(*Opposite below*) Taking part in a training exercise in the United States pre-Pearl Harbor is this US Army M3A1 Scout Car. As with the M3 Scout Car, it was armed with three machine guns; a single large-calibre machine gun and two small-calibre machine guns. Unlike the air-cooled shield-protected small-calibre machine guns on the M3 Scout Car, those on the M3A1 Scout Car pictured are water-cooled and lack an armoured shield. (*Patton Museum*)

(*Above*) In this picture of a radio-equipped US Army M3A1 Scout Car we can see that the rear door from the M3 Scout Car was dispensed with. Visible is the skate rail upon which the pintle-mounted machine guns of the vehicle were moved about. Due to the size of the radio mounted in the vehicle pictured, the two small-calibre machine guns normally fitted are not present. (*Patton Museum*)

(*Opposite above*) A restored M3A1 Scout Car and M5A1 Light Tank. The M3A1 was powered by an 87hp engine that provided it a maximum speed on level roads of 50mph. It was able to cross a trench 1.5 feet wide, and climb over a vertical wall a foot high. Maximum fording depth of the M3A1 Scout Car was 28 inches. (*Michael Green*)

(*Above*) The US Army continued to tinker with the design of the M3A1 Scout Car throughout its service career to improve its performance, and to see if it might be suitable for other roles. One of those proposed roles involved mounting a 37mm anti-tank gun on the vehicle, as seen in this picture. In this configuration it was designated the M3A1E3. However, testing proved the concept was not viable and the experiment was cancelled. (*TACOM*)

(*Opposite below*) The T2 Observation Post Tender weighed 5,800lbs empty and was intended to be manned by a crew of three. Power for the vehicle came from a 90hp engine, which provided it a maximum speed on level roads of 55mph. The front of the vehicle was protected by armour 0.375-inch thick and the side by armour 0.25-inch thick. It failed to impress the US Army and was never placed into series production. (*TACOM*)

The more fanciful wheeled AFV proposed to the pre-Pearl Harbor US Army was referred to as the 'Baker jumping vehicle'. It was to come in either an eight-wheel or four-wheel version. It was thought that its suspension system would allow it to hurl itself over obstacles of a certain size. Wiser heads soon prevailed and it never progressed past the wooden model stage, as seen in this picture. *(Patton Museum)*

The introduction of the 0.25-ton 'Jeep' into US Army service as a reconnaissance vehicle in 1941 prompted the Ordnance Department to test the concept of providing it with a certain degree of armour protection. Pictured is the first test unit labelled as the T25 Scout Car. As is evident in the picture, the armour protection was confined to the front of the vehicle. *(TACOM)*

The pre-Pearl Harbor testing of the T25 Scout Car by the Ordnance Department was not positive and it went nowhere. However, wartime requests by the user community pushed the Ordnance Department to revisit the concept of an armoured jeep. This would result in the T25E1 Scout Car, the T25E2 Scout Car (pictured), and the T25E3 Scout Car. As before, the concept was not practical and the programme was eventually cancelled. (TACOM)

The cancellation of the T25 series Scout Cars did not deter those soldiers in the combat zones of operations from going ahead and developing their own improvised armour kits. Pictured is an example of one of those home-made armoured jeeps of the 82nd Airborne Division operating near La Gleize, Belgium, on 18 January 1945. (Patton Museum)

ARMORED CAR T13   11-14-42

(*Opposite above*) In this picture we see a restored wartime US Army Jeep at a military vehicle collectors' meet. The owner has fitted it out as a copy of one of the many improvised armour kits added to Jeeps in Western Europe by US Army soldiers during the last two years of the Second World War. (*Christophe Vallier*)

(*Above*) In early 1941, an eight-wheeled vehicle fitted with a state-of-the-art independent suspension system was tested by the Ordnance Department, which labelled it as the T13 Armored Car. The firm that designed the vehicle was named the Trackless Tank Corporation and originally marketed it as a possible replacement for fully-tracked AFVs. (*TACOM*)

(*Opposite below*) With America's official entry into the Second World War in December 1941, the Ordnance Department had the chassis of the T13 Armored Car lengthened and equipped with larger wheels. It was also fitted with an open-topped turret armed with a 37mm main gun and two small-calibre machine guns, as seen in this picture, and relabelled as the Armored Car T13. (*TACOM*)

The Ordnance Department's early testing of the T13 Armored Car was not positive. Although the manufacturer submitted an improved version of the vehicle which addressed the design flaws uncovered in the initial testing, the Ordnance Department had already made up its mind and the T13 Armored Car programme, as well as related vehicles based on its chassis, were all cancelled. (*TACOM*)

Chapter Two

Second World War Wheeled AFVs

The successful employment of armoured cars in the reconnaissance role by both the British Army and German armies during the fighting in North Africa in 1940 and 1941 generated an interest within the US Army for similar vehicles. As a result, American industry was tasked in July 1941 with the design and development of a number of dedicated medium and heavy armoured cars.

It was the thickness of the armour on the vehicles that defined the difference between medium and heavy armoured cars, and not their weight. With that being said, the thicker the armour the heavier a vehicle would be. In July 1941, the plan called for the medium and heavy armoured cars selected for production to be suitable for employment by both the American and British armies. None would be ready for testing until 1942.

American Industry Responses

To answer the call for a medium armoured car, both the Ford Motor Company and the Chevrolet Division of the General Motors Corporation submitted vehicles for testing. The Ordnance Department had assumed responsibility for setting the requirements for all US Army wheeled and tracked vehicles, testing, design and their procurement in August 1941.

The Ford medium armoured car was labelled the T17 and was a 6 × 6. The General Motors vehicle referred to as the T17E1 Medium Armored Car was a 4 × 4. Both had the same 37mm main gun-armed turret designed by the Rock Island Arsenal. The 6 × 6 T17 prototypes impressed the US Army to such an extent that there was an order placed for 2,260 units of the vehicle in January 1942. A second order for an additional 1,500 units was authorized in June 1942.

An Overseer Appears

To manage the large numbers of AFVs being considered for production, both wheeled and tracked, the Ordnance Department formed the Special Armored Vehicle Board in late 1942. One of its tasks was to determine the US Army's requirement for armoured cars. Those not meeting certain requirements were to be cancelled to rationalize series production.

At the time that the Special Armored Vehicle Board was formed, the various members of the user community had different opinions on what type of armoured cars they wanted and how they would be employed. This difference of opinion was due to the mission diversity of the intended users, which included the Cavalry Branch of the US Army, and the US Army Armored Force and Tank Destroyer Force.

After evaluating the T17 Armored Car, the Special Armored Vehicle Board cancelled the orders for the vehicle. The Board believed that tracks were more suitable for vehicles with a gross weight exceeding 14,000lbs, due to their superior off-road performance. The T17 had a combat-loaded weight of 32,000lbs.

To help Ford keep the production lines going, the US Army Special Armored Vehicle Board authorized Ford to produce 250 units of the T17 for the British Army, who had already assigned it the name 'Deerhound'. However, on reviewing the US Army's test-data, the British Army rejected them, and thus none ever went overseas.

An unknown number of the T17 Medium Armored Cars (with their weapons removed) would be allocated to US Army Military Police units serving within the United States during the Second World War.

The General Motors Product

US Army testing of the smaller and lighter 4 × 4 General Motors prototype T17E1 went reasonably well, with some minor design issues being quickly corrected. At that point in time, the US Army was considering standardizing the T17E1 as the Medium Armored Car M6.

The T17E1 weighed 30,705lbs when combat loaded. Despite being a more reliable vehicle than the T17, the Special Armored Vehicle Board felt the T17E1 was also too large and heavy for a reconnaissance vehicle and cancelled it in December 1942. The British Army remained interested in the T17E1 and the Ordnance Department authorized General Motors to build the vehicle for them. The British Army assigned the name 'Staghound' to the T17E1.

Different Suspension System

The design and construction of two medium armoured cars fitted with an independent suspension system was authorized in January 1942. They were both built by the Chevrolet Division of General Motors and designated the T19 and the T19E1. Most previous American military armoured cars and scout cars had employed commercial truck suspension systems, fitted with leaf springs.

As could be expected, the off-road mobility of the T19 and T19E1 medium armoured cars was outstanding, with their independent suspension systems. The US Army recommended that future armoured cars be fitted with independent suspension systems. However, both greatly exceeded the weight limit set by the Special Armored Vehicle Board. Like all the other medium and heavy armoured cars submitted for consideration by the US Army, neither was approved.

As a test, a large turret armed with a 75mm main gun was mounted on the chassis of the Medium Armored Car T19E1 in November 1942. The combination was designated the T66 tank destroyer. There was British Army interest in the vehicle at first. However, like the T55 and T55E1, the Tank Destroyer Force quickly cancelled the T66 when it was clear that full-tracked tank destroyers had much better off-road mobility.

Heavy Armored Car

Besides the two different types of medium armoured cars submitted to the Ordnance Department for testing in 1942 by American industry, a heavy armoured car appeared. It was labelled the T18 and was an 8 × 8 vehicle. The builder was the Truck and Coach Division of General Motors, which began in-house testing of the first example in July 1942.

Originally intended to be fitted with the same 37mm main gun armed turret that went on the T17 and T17E1, British Army combat experience in early 1942 showed that the T18 would be under-gunned. This resulted in the second example of the vehicle being armed with a British-designed 57mm anti-tank gun and designated as the T18E2. The vehicle's combat loaded weight was 53,000lbs.

As could be surmised, both the T18 and T18E2 were too large and heavy for the Special Armored Vehicle Board and were rejected for use by the US Army in December 1942. The British Army still saw a need for the T18E2 and at one point had envisioned ordering 2,500 units. As testing of the vehicle went forward and design problems became more evident, the British Army eventually reduced its order to only thirty units, which it named the 'Boarhound'.

Even as General Motors was building the first example of the T18, armed with a 37mm main gun, it offered the US Army a 6 × 6 heavy armoured car. The proposed vehicle was designated the T18E1. The US Army was not interested and the project never got off the drawing board.

Stop-Gap Tank Destroyer

In early 1941, the US Army decided it needed a wheeled tank destroyer armed with a 37mm anti-tank gun as quickly as possible. The Chrysler Corporation responded by mounting an armoured-shield protected 37mm anti-tank gun in the rear cargo bay of an unarmoured 0.75-ton 4 × 4 truck. It was labelled the M6 Gun Motor Carriage (GMC). Hereafter, all GMCs will be referred to as 'tank destroyers'.

Series production of the M6 tank destroyer began in April 1942, with Chrysler building 5,380 units of the vehicle by October 1942. It was intended strictly as an interim design, until a better thought out wheeled tank destroyer could be developed and fielded. Despite being a stop-gap design, the M6 would be deployed to North Africa beginning in November 1942, during Operation Torch.

An observer of the M6 in North Africa stated the following in a March 1943 US Army report: 'The sending of such a patently inadequate [tank] destroyer into combat can be best termed a tragic mistake.' In an After-Action Report (AAR) titled *Operations of the 1st Armored in Tunisia*, Major General E.N. Harmon stated: 'The 37mm self-propelled gun, mounted on the 0.75-ton truck, is positively worthless and has never been used in this division.'

Rejected Wheeled Tank Destroyers

A number of experimental wheeled tank destroyers were also tested by the Ordnance Department but eventually rejected. There was the T14, an open-topped 6 × 6 armoured vehicle based on Jeep components armed with a 37mm anti-tank gun. Another was the T33, also armed with a shield-protected 37mm anti-tank gun, but mounted on an unarmoured 0.75-ton 4 × 4 Ford truck. It was later up-gunned with a shield-protected 57mm anti-tank gun and re-designated as the T44.

The need to mount an anti-tank gun of sufficient power to penetrate the armour on German medium tanks led to the US Army testing an open-topped armoured vehicle armed with a forward-firing 3-inch anti-tank gun. The 8 × 8 vehicle was designated the T55, with a modified second version being labelled the T55E1.

Both the T55 and T55E1 had been designed and built by the Cook Brothers Company, and hence were nicknamed 'The Cook Interceptors'. Ordnance Department testing of new full-tracked tank destroyers quickly demonstrated that they possessed superior off-road mobility to large, wheeled tank destroyers, and the T55 and T55E1 were soon cancelled.

The M6 Replacement

In July 1941, the US Army began searching for a replacement for the M6 tank destroyer. American industry was therefore asked to submit five candidate vehicles, for testing by the Ordnance Department, which had already laid out the general design parameters of the vehicle. All five candidate vehicles would be fitted with the same two-man turret armed with a 37mm main gun, then the primary anti-tank weapon in the US Army inventory.

The first of these new wheeled tank destroyers to arrive in March 1942 for testing by the Ordnance Department was a 6 × 6 Ford product designated the T22 tank destroyer. That same month, the US Army relabelled it and the other four candidate vehicles, not yet delivered for testing by the Ordnance Department, as light armoured cars, rather than as tank destroyers.

This change in titles reflected the fact that British Army combat experience gained in North Africa in early 1942 clearly demonstrated that a 37mm anti-tank gun was no longer adequate on the modern battlefield. However, fitted on a reconnaissance vehicle it offered enough firepower for its intended role as envisioned by the US Army at that time.

A Winner is Chosen

By early 1942, the US Army was desperate for an affordable light armoured car that could be built quickly, and in large numbers. Because the T22 performed so well during its initial testing period with the Ordnance Department, almost all concerned with the project agreed that with some minor modifications it should be quickly standardized and placed into production.

The T22 would be rushed through development by the US Army despite the fact that four other candidate vehicles had not yet even been delivered for testing. These included a Ford-designed and built 4 × 4 labelled the T22E1. The Fargo Division of General Motors had submitted two vehicles, the 6 × 6 T23 and the 4 × 4 T23E1.

The modified version of the T22 chosen by the US Army for production was designated the T22E2. In May 1942, Ford was awarded a contract to build the T22E2, which was standardized as the Light Armored Car M8 in June 1942. Combat loaded, the vehicle weighed 17,400lbs; un-stowed, it weighed 14,500lbs.

The decision to order the M8 Light Armored Car into production was later concurred upon by the Special Armored Vehicle Board, which believed that despite some design flaws, and being a bit heavier then desired, it was the best available vehicle at that time.

Production

Due to unresolved contract issues between the US Army and Ford, production of the M8 Light Armored Car did not begin until March 1943. Prior to that time, a number of modifications were made to the vehicle's design. These included the replacement of the original cast armour turret with a new welded armoured turret. Improvements were also made to the vehicle's front suspension system.

By the time production of the M8 ended in May 1945, a total of 8,532 units had been completed. A total of 1,205 units of the vehicle would be allocated to Lend-Lease, with the largest number going to the Free French Army, which received 689 units. In British Army service the vehicle was assigned the name 'Greyhound'.

Employment

The majority of M8 Light Armored Cars would serve with US Army mechanized cavalry units during the Second World War. They were organic to armoured divisions and tank destroyer battalions, but non-organic to infantry divisions. Post-war, the US Army did away with the title mechanized cavalry and simply referred to those units tasked with the reconnaissance mission as the 'cavalry', or just the 'CAV'.

From a 24 February 1944 War Department (the predecessor to the United States Department of Defense) manual titled *Cavalry Reconnaissance Troop (Mechanized)* comes this description of the M8 Light Armored Car and its role:

Armored Cars are the basic command and communication vehicles. The Light Armored Car, M8, is a 6 × 6 vehicle, weighs 16,400 pounds with equipment and crew, and is capable of cruising from 100 to 250 miles cross country or 200 to 400 miles on highways without refuelling. On a level, improved road, it can sustain a speed of 55 miles per hour. Each armoured car is equipped with a long-range radio set to assist in the exercise of command or for the purpose of relaying information received from subordinate elements to higher headquarters, and a short-range radio set for communication with a platoon, reconnaissance team or headquarters.

As the M8 Light Armored Car was designed with standard truck-type suspension components, to keep its cost down, its off-road performance was extremely limited. This fact was of great concern to many within the US Army prior to the vehicle being standardized and would remain a problem for many throughout the war years.

Major General Robert Crow, commander of the 6th Armored Division, so disliked the M8 Light Armored Car that he replaced them within his division, and even as his own command vehicle, with the full-tracked 75mm Howitzer Motor Carriage (HMC) M8.

From an After Action Report of the 640th Tank Destroyer Battalion that fought in the Philippines between January and March 1945 comes this comment: 'The M8s and M20s in reconnaissance companies proved to be very good reconnaissance vehicles over terrain where a road net existed, however, over difficult terrain their ability to reconnoitre for tracked vehicles is very limited.'

In contrast, Lieutenant Colonel Michael Popowski, who commanded an M8 Light Armored Car equipped unit in the Italian Theatre of Operations, stated in a 7 October 1944 US Army report these positive comments: 'During my combat experience I saw only one instance where the armoured car was not able to go where the tanks went … Some of its capabilities over a tracked vehicle are: quietness, range, maintenance, and weight, which are all important in reconnaissance.'

Despite some positive comments on the employment of the M8 and M20, the general consensus on the vehicle's merits were summed up in this statement by the Ordnance Department at the conclusion of the Second World War:

The armoured cars M8 and M20 had varied acceptance in this theatre [Western Europe]. However, on the whole, using organizations were not satisfied with the performance of these vehicles as they felt they were under-powered, lacked manoeuvrability, sufficient floatation for cross-country operation, and sufficient armoured protection. These vehicles were not reliable, resulting in excessive quantities dead-lined in maintenance shops for repair.

M8 Variant

The Tank Destroyer Command identified a need for a turret-less version of the M8 Light Armored Car. Their requirement was authorized and Ford was awarded a contract to build a vehicle that was designated as the Armored Utility Car M20.

The M20 Armored Utility Car was standardized in May 1943, and would serve in a number of roles, including command car, personnel carrier and cargo carrier. Ford began M20 production in July 1943; at the conclusion of production in June 1945, a total of 3,791 units had been manufactured.

Variants of the M8 Light Armored Car that were not placed into production included the Multiple-Gun Motor Carriage T69 and the Armored Chemical Car T30. The T69 featured an open-topped turret armed with four large-calibre machine guns. The T30 never made it off the drawing board. It would have consisted of a standard M8 Light Armored Car fitted with five 7-inch rocket launchers on either side of the vehicle's turret.

Rejected Designs

Despite not being invited by the US Army to provide a light armoured car for testing by the Ordnance Department, the Studebaker Corporation did so anyway. The 6 × 4 vehicle they submitted was labelled as the T43. With the acceptance of the M8 Light Armored Car for production, the Studebaker submission, as those provided by Ford and General Motors, never went past the prototype stage.

Another light armoured car that did not make it into production was a variant of the T14 tank destroyer. It had been requested by the Tank Destroyer Command and dubbed the Scout Car T24. It was approved for production by the Special Armored Vehicle Board, but it was disapproved at a higher level.

Proposed M8 Replacement

As a replacement for the M8 Light Armored Car, the Special Weapons Board recommended the development of another light armoured car of the same size and weight, but fitted with an independent suspension system.

As a result of the US Army's interest, Studebaker submitted an 8 × 6 vehicle labelled the T27 Light Armored Car. The Chevrolet Division of General Motors submitted a 6 × 6 vehicle, assigned the designation T28 Light Armored Car. Testing of these two experimental light armoured cars showed that both had superior off-road performance to the M8.

Of the two proposed replacements for the M8 Light Armored Car, the off-road performance of the T28 was superior to its 8 × 6 counterpart the T27. This resulted in any additional development of the T27 being cancelled.

There also arose a call for standardizing the T28 as the Light Armored Car M38 in December 1944, once necessary modifications were made to the vehicle's design. The vehicle combat-loaded weighed 15,300lbs. The end of the Second World War in August 1945 resulted in cancellation of the vehicle before production could commence.

(*Above*) With America's official entry into the Second World War, there was a frantic effort to greatly increase the number of wheeled and tracked AFVs being built. This resulted in a push to field light, medium and heavy armoured cars that would meet both US and British Army requirements. Pictured is the Ford-designed contender for a medium armoured car that the Ordnance Department labelled the T17. (*TACOM*)

(*Opposite above*) In the March 1942 Table of Organization and Equipment (TO&E) proposed for US Army armoured divisions, there was a requirement for forty-nine armoured cars to perform reconnaissance duties. What had not been decided at that time was what type of armoured car would be acquired as all were still in development, including the Ford-designed T17 medium armoured car pictured here. (*TACOM*)

(*Opposite below*) The other contender for supplying the US and British Army with a suitable medium armoured car was the General Motors Corporation, which provided a vehicle designated the T17E1 seen here. The vehicle had some advanced design features such as an automatic transmission, but still rode on commercial truck axles and leaf springs, which greatly hindered its off-road mobility. (*TACOM*)

(*Above*) The large external fuel drum visible on this unrestored General Motors Corporation T17E1 Medium Armored Car pilot also existed on the other side of the vehicle. This was a British Army requirement to increase the range of the vehicle, which reflected its experience gained fighting the Axis in North Africa. The approximate cruising range of the T17E1 on roads was 450 miles. (*Chris Hughes*)

(*Opposite above*) The pilot model of the General Motors Corporation T17E1 Medium Armored Car seen here lacked the small rounded opening for the 2-inch smoke mortar that appeared on the right front of the turret roof on series production units of the vehicle. Advanced features of the vehicle included an automatic transmission and power steering. (*TACOM*)

(*Opposite below*) A series production model of the T17E1 Medium Armored Car, which was named the 'Staghound' by the British Army. It lacks the large pistol ports that were seen on either side of the turrets on the pilot units of the vehicle. The vehicle had a height of 9 feet 3 inches, a length of 18 feet, and width of 8 feet 8 inches. (*TACOM*)

(*Above*) In the markings of the postwar Belgian Army is a restored example of a series production T17E1 Medium Armored Car. Power for the vehicle was provided by two commercial truck engines that each produced 95hp, giving the vehicle a top speed on level roads of 55mph. The vehicle was able to cross a trench 1.5 feet in width, climb over a vertical wall 21 inches high, and had a maximum fording depth of 32 inches. (*Michael Krauss*)

(*Opposite above*) An anti-aircraft variant of the T17E1 Medium Armored Car built and tested in the United States per a British Army request. It was designated the T17E2 by the Ordnance Department. The British Army named it the 'Staghound AA' (anti-aircraft). It was armed with two air-cooled large-calibre machine guns mounted in a power-operated turret. (*TACOM*)

(*Opposite below*) Another variant of the T17E1 Medium Armored Car built and tested in the United States per a British Army request. It was designated as the T17E3 by the Ordnance Department and consisted of the turret of the US Army 75mm Howitzer Motor Carriage M8 mounted on the chassis of the standard T17E1 Medium Armored Car. (*TACOM*)

(*Opposite above*) In January 1942 the US Army authorized the funding for the development and testing of the Medium Armored Car T19. In contrast to the commercial truck-type suspension systems on the T17 and T17E1 Medium Armored Cars, the T19 was fitted with an independent suspension system. Except for its suspension system it was very similar to the T17 and T17E1 Medium Armored Cars. (*TACOM*)

(*Opposite below*) Testing of the T19 Medium Armored Car began in October 1942. These tests led to the construction of a modified version of the T19, pictured here, labelled as the T19E1 Medium Armored Car. The T19E1 was fitted with the powertrain of the US Army's M5 Light Tank, which included two Cadillac engines as well as an automatic transmission. (*TACOM*)

(*Above*) Pictured during off-road testing is the T19E1 Medium Armored Car. It had a redesigned and lighter turret than that mounted on the T19, but was still armed with a 37mm main gun. The independent suspension systems on the T19 and T19E1s proved far superior to the commercial truck-based suspension systems found on other US Army armoured cars. (*TACOM*)

There was a single variant of the T19E1 chassis as seen here. It was labelled as the T66 75mm Gun Motor Carriage, which was a tank destroyer by any other name. The vehicle had been proposed by the US Army in November 1942, but cancelled in March 1943 along with the T19 and T19E1 Medium Armored Cars. (*TACOM*)

Once considered for use by both the US and British Army was the T18E2 Heavy Armored Car. Named the 'Boarhound' by the British Army, it was armed with a 57mm main gun. Series production of the four-man vehicle began in December 1942, with two being built that month. A total of thirty were completed by May 1943 before being cancelled. (*TACOM*)

Despite the cancellation of the T18E2 Heavy Armored Car by the US Army, the British Army continued to express interest in the vehicle and eventually all thirty built were shipped to Great Britain under Lend Lease. Other than some testing, the British Army decided that it would not be committed to combat. (*TACOM*)

The US Army began a crash programme in early 1941 to develop and quickly field as many stop-gap wheeled tank destroyers as possible. One of these lines of development led to the fielding of the M6 seen here. It was officially labelled by the US Army as a gun motor carriage. The only armour on the vehicle was the shield that protected the 37mm anti-tank gun and its crew. (*TACOM*)

ARMORED CAR T-22

(*Opposite above*) When first conceived it remained unclear to the US Army if the shield-protected 37mm anti-tank gun on the M6 tank destroyer would be better suited to fire over the front or rear of the vehicle. Testing quickly led to the conclusion that the gun aimed to the rear was a better choice, as the muzzle blast from the weapon when fired over the front of vehicle was too hard on the driver. (*TACOM*)

(*Opposite below*) A truly novel approach to mounting an anti-tank gun, supposedly of sufficient size to deal with German medium tanks, was the 3-inch GMC that was designated as the T55E1. It and an earlier version labelled the T55 were both tested in 1943, but neither could match the off-road mobility of fully-tracked armoured vehicles armed with the same weapon and were therefore rejected by the US Army. (*TACOM*)

(*Above*) In the summer of 1941, in pursuit of a next-generation wheeled tank destroyer to replace the stop-gap M6 GMC, the US Army solicited proposals from two different companies to see what they could come up with. By the time the first candidate vehicle arrived for testing, the Ford T22 (pictured) and the yet-to-be-delivered candidate vehicles were all re-labelled as light armoured cars. (*TACOM*)

(*Opposite above*) The US Army felt the Ford T22 Light Armored Car had a lot of potential, and by tweaking the design a bit they came up with another pilot model of the vehicle designated as the T22E2. It was this pilot vehicle that the US Army decided to standardize as the M8 Light Armored Car; a restored example is pictured. (*Christophe Vallier*)

(*Opposite below*) A major design difference between the T22E2 Light Armored Cars and the majority of series production M8 Light Armored Cars was the latter's welded open-topped turret. The open-topped turrets on the T22E2 and the very early series production M8 were castings. Notice the bracket between the front and rear wheel fenders for the storage of three anti-tank mines, seen on this restored example. (*Christophe Vallier*)

(*Above*) Reflecting the very thin armour on the M8 Light Armored Car, the thickest portion being the gun shield at one inch, the crew of this vehicle has added a large number of sandbags to the front hull. The sandbags are held in place by a supporting bracket of the front hull. The driver has a sub-machine gun at the ready for any close-in threat to the vehicle. (*Patton Museum*)

An overhead shot of a series production M8 Light Armored Car, with its crew of four. Due to the small size of the vehicle's turret, the vehicle commander doubled as the loader for the 37mm main gun. There was storage space for eighty rounds of 37mm ammunition on the M8. It was 16 feet 5 inches long, 8 feet 4 inches in width and had a height of 7 feet 4 inches. (*TACOM*)

This M8 Light Armored Car is on patrol in the Netherlands in September 1944. It is armed with a large-calibre machine gun fitted to a ring mount, allowing the operator to traverse the weapon 360 degrees. Also visible is the coaxial small-calibre machine gun fitted alongside the 37mm main gun. (*Patton Museum*)

Due to the extremely cramped nature of the turret on the M8 Light Armored Car, the vehicle commander some-times would aim and fire its large-calibre turret-mounted machine gun from outside the confines of the vehicle's turret. Armor thickness on the vehicle's turret, not including the gun shield, was only 19mm. (*Patton Museum*)

Sporting the remains of a lime whitewash winter camouflage scheme is a US Army M8 Light Armored Car in Belgium during the Battle of the Bulge. The upper front hull armour on the vehicle was 16mm thick, and the lower front hull 19mm. The hull sides of the M8 were only 9mm thick. There was no armour on the hull floor on the vehicle, which led crews to often line the bottom floor of the vehicle's crew compartment with sandbags. (*Patton Museum*)

(*Above*) The Ordnance Department believed the various ring mounts employed on the M8 Light Armored Car for the vehicle's turret-mounted large-calibre machine gun lacked the necessary strength and durability. The end result was the fielding in late 1943 of a new pintle bracket mount for the large-calibre turret-mounted machine gun fitted to the rear of the vehicle's turret, as pictured. (*TACOM*)

(*Opposite above*) As seen in this official Ordnance Department picture, the new pintle bracket mount for the large-calibre turret-mounted machine gun on late series production M8 Light Armored Cars could be folded down. The exposed external bracket that once held three anti-tank mines on either side of the vehicle has been replaced by a large unarmoured storage bin. (*TACOM*)

(*Opposite below*) The Tank Destroyer Command of the US Army issued a requirement for two wheeled vehicles, both to be based on the M8 Light Armored Car chassis. One was to be an armoured command car and the other an armoured personnel carrier, which could also do double-duty as an ammunition carrier. Ford decided that only one vehicle was needed and came up with the T26 Armoured Utility Vehicle, pictured here. (*TACOM*)

(*Opposite above*) The US Army concurred with Ford that the T26 Armored Utility Vehicle could satisfy both of the Tank Destroyer Command's requirements, and went ahead and eventually standardized it as the M20 Armored Utility Vehicle. A restored example is pictured. Notice that the bracket for supporting the ring mount for the large-calibre machine gun is different from that on the T26. (*Michael Green*)

(*Opposite below*) A restored example of an M20 Armored Utility Vehicle owned by a private collector. The vehicle was originally designated as the M10 Armored Utility Vehicle by the Ordnance Department. However, this caused confusion when it was assigned to tank destroyer units equipped with the M10 Tank Destroyer. This pushed the Ordnance Department to re-label it as the M20. (*Michael Green*)

(*Above*) Taken somewhere in Western Europe is this picture of an M20 Armored Utility Vehicle. Notice the improvised ring-mount for the large-calibre machine gun. Not all M20s were fitted with ring mounts and their associated weapons, as many were only employed in rear area duties. The open top arrangement of the design meant that many units made improvised canvas shelters for the vehicles as protection from inclement weather. (*Patton Museum*)

In search of a better ring mount for the M8 Light Armored Car and the M20 Armored Utility Vehicle, the Ordnance Department developed the T86 Ring Mount. Rather than test its durability with a single large-calibre machine gun, the Ordnance Department borrowed a twin large-calibre machine gun from the US Navy, as pictured. It must have passed its tests as it eventually resulted in the M66 Ring Mount, which appeared on late production M20s. (*TACOM*)

A rejected variant of the M8 Light Armored Car was the T69 Multiple Gun Motor Carriage. It was optimized as an anti-aircraft vehicle but could have also been used in a ground support role. Its one-man turret was armed with four large-calibre machine guns. Testing of the vehicle did not go well and the US Army decided to stick with its half-track-based anti-aircraft vehicles. (*TACOM*)

Despite not being asked by the Ordnance Department to submit a pilot vehicle in its quest for a suitable light armoured car, the Studebaker Corporation went ahead and submitted a vehicle anyway, seen here, that the Ordnance Department designated as the T21. The decision by the US Army to go forward with a modified version of the Ford T22 design meant the Studebaker project never went anywhere. (TACOM)

The T24 Scout Car was something the Tank Destroyer Command saw a requirement for in early 1942. It was based on the same design as a proposed tank destroyer that the Ordnance Department had labelled as the 37mm Gun Motor Carriage T14. In the end, neither vehicle was approved for series production. (TACOM)

Well aware of the design limitations of the commercial truck-type suspension system on the M8 Light Armored Car, the Ordnance Department indicated to private industry a desire to see a next-generation replacement for the M8, which would feature an independent suspension system. The Studebaker submission designated as the T27 Light Armored Car is pictured. (*TACOM*)

The General Motors Corporation contender for an M8 Light Armored Car replacement. It was labelled as the Light Armored Car T28 by the Ordnance Department. Testing of the Studebaker T27 alongside the General Motors T28 led to the conclusion that the latter was the superior vehicle and should be approved for series production by the US Army as quickly as possible. (*TACOM*)

Once approved for standardization by the US Army, the General Motors T28 was re-designated as the Light Armored Car M38. Such was the anticipation that the vehicle would quickly be placed into production, the British Army assigned it the name 'Wolfhound'. With the end of the war in Europe in May 1945, the M38 was cancelled before production commenced. (TACOM)

A one-of-a-kind wheeled AFV employed by the US Army Air Forces during the Second World War that was not designed and built in the United States is the S-1 Scout Car. It was an Australian-designed armoured body mounted on a 4 × 4 military cargo truck chassis. It was intended to be used to guard American air bases in Australia, and it is reported that approximately forty were built. (TACOM)

Chapter Three

Cold War Wheeled AFVs

The subpar performance of the M8 Light Armored Car and M20 Armored Utility Cars during the Second World War did much to sour the US Army on the usefulness of such vehicles. The general post-war consensus within the US Army was that full-tracked AFVs were much more useful on a wider variety of terrain and missions. This meant that what funding was available post-war was primarily directed at the development of full-tracked AFVs.

During the Korean War, the US Army only employed a small number of M8s and M20s in rear area security operations. Shortly after the Korean War, the US Army retired all of its remaining M8s and M20s, except a small number which lingered on for a few more years with US Army National Guard units. Upon the departure of the last Second World War era M8 Light Armored Car, the term armoured car passed from use by the American military.

A Need Appears

Despite the general aversion by the US Army to wheeled AFVs in the immediate post-war period, a few research and development projects on such vehicles were pursued. Except for one wooden mockup, none would ever leave the drawing board. Things began to change, however, in the mid-1950s, as the United States became more involved in what would eventually become known to Americans as the Vietnam War.

As the United States Government sought to prop-up the South Vietnamese Government, there arose a need by the Army of the Republic of South Vietnam (ARVN) for a new wheeled AFV to perform convoy security duties. At that time, the ARVN was using the Second World War vintage M8 Light Armored Car for that role. A number of these had been left behind by the French Army when it departed that region in 1956.

An Interim Wheeled AFV

Because the US Army had no wheeled AFVs in its inventory, or any even in development, and time was of the essence, it began looking around for a commercial-off-the-shelf (COTS) wheeled AFV that might fit the bill. In a timely coincidence, the

Terra-Space Corporation, a division of the Cadillac Gage Company, had developed and built a prototype of a machine gun armed wheeled 4 x 4 AFV, which the firm named the 'V-100 Commando'.

The initial prototype of the V-100 Commando appeared in late 1962. Cadillac Gage had intended to market it to Third World armies of limited means and maintenance abilities that might be unable to handle more expensive and complex full-tracked AFVs. As far as the US Army was concerned, this perfectly described the ARVN, and two prototypes were shipped to South Vietnam in 1963 for testing.

The V-100 hull was of dedicated design but to keep its costs down it was intended to utilize as many existing commercial and military components as possible. It was never intended as a reconnaissance vehicle like the M8 Light Armored Car; rather it was envisioned as an internal security vehicle for Third World armies.

After some fits and starts, the V-100 was designated as the XM706 by the US Army. It entered into ARVN service in 1965. That was the same year the US Government committed American ground combat units to the Vietnam War; prior to this time it had only been American military advisors, who were not supposed to engage in combat operations.

Among the many supporting units to arrive in South Vietnam in 1965 were US Army military police. Tasked with guarding US Army supply convoys and having observed the success that the ARVN were having with the American-supplied XM706, they managed to borrow six examples for testing in mid-1967.

The American Military Versions

Positive results with the six borrowed ARVN XM706s led the US Army to request production of a modified version of the vehicle, labelled as the XM706E1, for its military police units. Due to manufacturing problems at Cadillac Gage, the first production XM706E1s did not arrive in South Vietnam until late 1968. Between mid-1967 and late 1968, the US Army borrowed XM706s from the ARVN as an interim measure.

There was also an open-top machine gun armed version of the XM706E1, designated the XM706E2. It was built for use by US Air Force personnel guarding air bases in South Vietnam, which proved popular targets for the enemy throughout the American military presence in that country, which lasted until 1973.

With the American military drawdown in South Vietnam, which began in 1970, the majority of XM706s and XM706E2s would be returned to the United States. The XM706E1 was finally standardized by the US Army as the M706 in 1971.

The US Army was unable to envision any need for the M706 following the end of the Vietnam War in 1975. The vehicle was employed in a number of secondary roles, including guarding US Army bases, being modified for use as simulated Soviet/Eastern Bloc vehicles or destroyed as range targets.

Makeshift Wheeled AFVs Appear

Due to a lack of sufficient wheeled or tracked AFVs to provide protection for American military truck convoys, US Army military police units began adding improvised armour to their M151 series 0.25-ton trucks. Eventually, the US Army went ahead and built two standard add-on armour kits for the vehicles.

US Army and USMC transportation unit personnel also decided to take matters into their own hands, and in 1967 began to arm and armour some of their 6 × 6 cargo trucks, turning them into make-shift wheeled AFVs, popularly referred to as 'gun trucks'.

Without a template, the resulting unauthorized machine-gun armed gun trucks came in a wide array of shapes and sizes, based on whatever material and weapons were at hand. Some series production armouring kits developed by the US Army eventually made it to the field, beginning in 1967.

The typical platform for the great majority of gun trucks was the standard US Army/USMC M54 5-ton cargo truck or the smaller M35 2.5-ton cargo truck. With the end of American military involvement in the Vietnam War, the surviving gun trucks were no doubt returned to their original configuration as cargo trucks, except for a single example on display at Fort Eustis Transportation Museum.

Rejected Wheeled AFVs

In the 1960s, the Lockheed Missile and Space Company came up with an 8 × 8 articulated vehicle for the US Army's consideration. The company name for the vehicle was the 'Twister'. The US Army tested three prototypes of the Twister in 1970. One was armoured and fitted with a 20mm automatic cannon. It was designated the XM808, but not adopted by the US Army.

In the early 1970s, the US Army began entertaining proposals for a wheeled or full-tracked armoured reconnaissance vehicle. The official title of the project was the Armored Reconnaissance Scout Vehicle (ARSV). Lockheed submitted a 6 × 6 version of the XM808, which was referred to as the XM800W. It too was armed with a 20mm automatic cannon. Due to rising costs, the ARSV programme was cancelled in 1975.

Odd Man Out

In the mid-1970s, the Verne Corporation developed a 4 × 4 wheeled AFV series they originally labelled as the AM300, and later renamed the 'Dragoon 300'. The series did not enjoy much sales success with the American military, except for a 1983 US Navy purchase of a small number to guard its nuclear weapon sites. Pictorial evidence shows that the US Army employed at least one example of the Dragoon 300 in an experimental role in the early 1980s.

The XM706E1 Post Vietnam War Replacement

The US Air Force would continue to employ the XM706E1 for guarding air bases and Intercontinental Ballistic Missile (ICBM) sites for a number of years before replacing the vehicle with a simpler and more affordable product they labelled the 'Peace-keeper'. The vehicle had the provision for mounting a small-calibre machine gun on the roof of its superstructure. Protection for the gunner was provided by a gun shield.

Like the XM706E2, the Peacekeeper was designed and built by Cadillac Gage. The company trade name for the vehicle was the 'Commando Ranger'. It was not a dedicated design like the XM706E2, rather it was an improvised design based upon a 4 × 4 Chrysler pickup truck chassis. The US Navy also adopted the Peacekeeper, which was used by USMC units guarding submarine bases or escorting shipments of nuclear missiles from storage sites to submarines in port. By the 1990s, these vehicles had outlived their service lives and most became range targets, with a few adopted by American police departments.

New Requirements

In February 1979, the pro-American Shah of Iran was deposed, and in November of that same year Iranian students seized the American Embassy and held hostage all those within. As the US Army's primary focus had been on the fielding of tank-heavy forces needed to stop a Soviet military invasion of Western Europe, it lacked the combat units that might have been employed to quickly respond to this turn of events.

The inability of the US Army to react to the unforeseen events in Iran in 1979 led to the formation in 1980 of the Rapid-Deployment Joint Task Force (RDJTF), later to become US Central Command (CENTCOM) in 1983. The RDJTF concluded that it would have to quickly organize ground forces, with the emphasis on rapid-deployment by existing US Air Force transport aircraft. This new emphasis dictated that any AFV chosen could not weigh more than 34,000lbs.

A Vehicle is Chosen

As the RDJTF felt that time was of the essence, it decided that the US Army and USMC would jointly explore the possibility of acquiring an existing off-the-shelf wheeled or tracked AFV design modified to serve the needs of both services. It was decided that this yet-to-be-selected AFV would be referred to as the Light Armored Vehicle (LAV).

The LAV would also act as an interim vehicle in lieu of the USMC acquiring a lightly-armoured full-tracked Mobile Protected Weapon System (MPWS), later referred to as the Advanced Combat Vehicle Technology (ACVT) Programme. The ACVT Programme was eventually cancelled.

Three firms submitted weapon-armed LAVs for testing, with the Diesel Division of General Motors providing the winning product in 1982. Their submission was a license-built copy of an 8 × 8 vehicle designed by the Swiss firm of Motorwagenfabrik AG (MOWAG) named 'Piranha I'. The first prototype of Piranha I appeared in 1972.

The US Army had originally envisioned ordering approximately 2,350 units of the LAV in two different versions. One was to be manned by a three-man crew and armed with a 25mm automatic cannon, with the other being an armoured personnel carrier armed only with a large-calibre machine gun.

The US Army was confident enough in its belief that it would soon be taking the 25mm automatic-cannon-equipped model of the LAV into the inventory that it went ahead and assigned it the designation M1047. Due to funding issues, the US Army dropped out of the LAV programme in 1984. However, the US Army would borrow eleven units of the LAV-25 for testing from the USMC, starting in 1986. Unhappy with their off-road capabilities, they were all returned in 1991.

The USMC decided to go forward with the LAV programme and received Congressional funding for 758 units of the vehicle. Unlike the US Army, which had anticipated taking into service only two different models of the LAV, the USMC ordered it in a number of different versions. Interestingly, it was the US Army Tank-automotive and Armaments Command (TACOM) rather than the USMC or the US Navy procurement-system that acquired the LAV family for the USMC.

LAV Models

The LAV family includes both offensively-oriented weapon carriers and those intended for supporting roles only. The offensively-oriented weapon carriers include the LAV-25 (25mm automatic-cannon-armed model), the LAV-AT (Anti-tank) armed with the TOW2 missile and the LAV-M (Mortar) armed with an 81mm mortar. The LAV-25 is the most numerous weapon carrier in the USMC inventory.

There was a fourth offensively-oriented weapon carrier version of the LAV family designated as the LAV-AD (Air Defense). The USMC had originally envisioned ordering 125 units of the LAV-AD, but a funding shortfall resulted in only 17 units being acquired. The vehicles were armed with surface-to-air missiles and a 25mm rotary cannon. All were placed into storage by 2004.

The support variants of the LAV family employed by the USMC include the LAV-L (Logistic Vehicle), the LAV-R (Recovery Vehicle), the LAV-C2 (Battalion Command and Control Vehicle), the LAV-MEWSS (Mobile Electronic-Warfare Support System Vehicle) and the newest, the LAV-JLNBCCRS (Joint Light Nuclear-Biological-Chemical-Reconnaissance Vehicle).

There were other variants of the LAV family proposed for production which for a variety of reasons never entered into service, such as an armoured personnel carrier (APC) and an ammo carrier. Also proposed was a version labelled the LAV-AG

(Assault Gun) armed with a 105mm main gun. However, since the development and fielding of the LAV-AD received higher funding priority, there were no funds available for the continued development of the LAV-AG.

Into Action

Originally envisioned for employment in the Middle East, the LAV family would first see combat during the American military invasion of Panama in December 1989, named Operation Just Cause. Their next combat action would occur during the short ground war portion of Operation Desert Storm in January 1991.

In consideration of its very thin armour protection, a USMC gunnery manual on the LAV-25 suggests ways in which the crew can make their vehicle more survivable on the battlefield as well as what types of enemy equipment pose the biggest threat:

> Smoke may also be used to keep the enemy from observing the vehicle. Minimizing the number of rounds fired from any position (primary, alternate) aids in confusing the enemy as to the LAV-25's exact location and aids in avoiding detection caused by firing signature. Generally, the most dangerous targets pose the following threats: Tanks at ranges of 2,000 metres [2,187 yards] are the greatest threat to LAV-25s. Within that range, the tank has a greater kill probability. At ranges greater than 2,000 metres, a BRDM, BMP, or helicopter firing ATGM [anti-tank guided missile] is the most dangerous threat. Helicopters, tanks, and BMPs, within their effective ranges, have greater kill probability against the LAV-25 than hand-held high-explosive anti-tank (HEAT) weapons (for example RPGs) within their effective ranges. Stationary vehicles deliver fire more accurately (and are therefore more dangerous) than moving vehicles.'

In a USMC report titled *Sand and Steel: Lessons Learned on US Marine Corps Armor and Anti-Armor Operations from the Gulf War* appears this passage by Captain Dennis Green. In it he describes why his LAVs managed to survive encounters with Iraqi tanks that in theory should have dominated the battlefield over the LAVs:

> Well, I think in a lot of ways we were lucky … Iraqis were real poor gunners; their gunnery skills just stunk. We could hit them at 3,000 metres [3,281 yards] with our main gun (25mm sabot). And they'd shoot at us with tanks at 3,000 metres and they couldn't hit us with tank fire, which is inherently more accurate. Bigger round, more stable than these (25mm) sabot rounds – they couldn't hit us. There are lots of reports – Charlie Company had some – pretty close encounters with tanks, and they just couldn't hit people.

The LAV family would go on to serve an important role during Operation Enduring Freedom, the American military invasion and occupation of Afghanistan, which lasted from 2001 to 2014. The LAV family then went on to take part in Operation Iraqi

Freedom, which began in 2003, and was followed by the Iraqi Insurgency that lasted until American combat units left the country in 2011.

LAV Upgrades

To address vehicle obsolescence, the USMC has put its LAV family through Service Life Extension Programmes (SLEPs), one of which resulted in the vehicle series being assigned the letter and number code 'A1'. The initial LAV-A1 configuration vehicle came off the rebuilding line in 2003 and the last in 2005.

Among the improvements that came with the LAV-A1 configuration were survivability features aimed at minimizing the vehicle's battlefield signature, both visual and thermal. This was not the first USMC attempt to improve the battlefield survivability of the LAV family. A small number of add-on armour kits were acquired in both 1991 and 1998.

In response to feedback from units employing the LAV family in Afghanistan and Iraq, in 2004 the USMC undertook the 'Survivability Upgrade I Program'. A description of the programme appears in an unclassified US Navy document:

> This upgrade became the LAV-A2 configuration standard, involved developing and installing a Ballistic Protection Upgrade Package (BPUP), power pack enhancements, upgraded suspension, and other modifications. The BPUP system consists of three kits, two of which provide additional protection from threats, while the third provides an internal and external stowage system.

The BPUP was aimed at providing the LAV family additional protection from threats to their front and sides. As originally designed, the armour was proof only against small-calibre machine-gun fire and small overhead artillery fragments. For additional protection, the LAV-A2 configuration includes an automatic fire suppression system.

To address the ever present threat posed by improvised explosive devices (IEDs), the LAV Programme Office developed an underbody blast-deflecting V-shaped armour kit, referred to as the (D-Kit). It was fielded in 2009 and is labelled as a 'Special Purpose Mission Kit', which meant it was to be applied to the LAV-A2 vehicles in theatre at the discretion of the operational commander.

Besides upgrading its existing inventory of the LAV-A1 family to the LAV-A2 configuration, the USMC ordered 281 new-built units of the LAV-A2, along with new-build electric-drive turrets to replace the existing hydraulically-operated turrets on its LAV-25 A2 fleet. The USMC is currently anticipating retaining the LAV-A2 family until 2035.

Specialized Wheeled AFV

The US Army was long aware that an important part of the Soviet/Eastern Bloc military arsenal consisted of nuclear, biological and chemical (NBC) weapons. To counter this threat, in 1990 the US Army ordered forty-eight units of a modified version of a West German Army chemical, biological radiological and nuclear (CBRN) wheeled reconnaissance vehicle from General Dynamics Land Systems.

In West German Army service, the 6 × 6 vehicle was referred to as the TPz Fuchs (Fox), and besides the CBRN variant came in a number of other models including an armoured personnel carrier (APC). In US Army service, the CBRN version of the TPz Fuchs (Fox) was standardized as the M93 Fox, Nuclear, Biological, Chemical Reconnaissance System (NBC-RS) vehicle.

The M93 Fox NBC-RS vehicles ordered by the US Army were not ready for service during Operation Desert Shield in 1990, the precursor to Operation Desert Storm in 1991. The West German Army therefore loaned the US Army sixty units from its own inventory for use during the conflict. These vehicles and new-built vehicles were eventually upgraded and assigned an 'A1' designation.

Due to its employment during Operation Iraq Freedom, and the follow-on insurgency, the M93A1 Fox NBC-RS was fitted with add-on armour kits. In addition, its original manually-operated small-calibre machine gun was replaced by a dismountable remote-control weapon station armed with a large-calibre machine gun. All of the US Army's M93A1 Fox NBC-RS vehicles were later upgraded and are now labelled as the M93A1P1 Fox NBC-RS.

In the early 1950s, the US Army evaluated a wooden mockup seen here of a proposed vehicle they labelled as the T115 Armored Wheeled Personnel Carrier. They were not impressed and decided in 1957 that a new fully-tracked AFV, designated as the M114 Command and Reconnaissance Carrier, was the better choice. (*TACOM*)

(*Opposite above*) The initial pilot model of the Cadillac Gage V-100 Commando armoured car. The US Army had not solicited its design and development but went ahead and tested the first three pilots in the early 1960s. The US Army was impressed enough to buy all three pilots, shipping two of the three off to South Vietnam for additional testing in 1963. (*TACOM*)

(*Opposite below*) The two pilot models of the Cadillac Gage V-100 Commando armoured car shipped to South Vietnam were assigned the designation XM706. Unlike the original pilot model of the V-100 Commando that was fitted with periscopes along either side of its hull, all subsequent pilots as well as production units had vision blocks, as seen here on this XM706. (*Patton Museum*)

(*Above*) The XM706 had two-piece doors on either side of its hull, as well as a two-piece door on the rear of the vehicle's hull that is visible in this picture. Early production units of the XM706 had angular cutouts for their wheels, with later production units having semicircular cutouts. The vehicle was amphibious without any prior preparation. (*Patton Museum*)

A XM706 in service with the Army of the Republic of South Vietnam (ARVN). It can be identified as an early production vehicle by the angular cutouts over the wheels and the tool bracket welded on to the left rear hull side of the vehicle. Later production units had this feature replaced by an engine access hatch. *(Patton Museum)*

Belonging to a private collector are a Second World War era M8 Light Armored Car in the foreground and behind it a Vietnam War era XM706. Late production units of the XM706 had only three vision blocks on the left side of the hull, while earlier production units of the vehicle had four. *(Michael Green)*

Eventually, the US Army would standardize the XM706 as the M706 after some minor redesigns. One of these features included a cover over the rear engine air intake grill, as seen on this preserved example of an M706. The vehicle is shown with the standard one-man manually-operated turret armed with two machine guns. *(Paul Hannah)*

During the Vietnam War, US Air Force Security Police units were equipped with the turretless XM706E2, seen here preserved at the US Air Force Museum. The need arose for the XM706E2 when the South Vietnamese Air Force proved unable to defend US Air Force bases in their country from enemy ground attacks. *(Air Force Museum)*

This Vietnam War era photograph shows a trio of US Air Force XM706E2s at an air base in South Vietnam. Notice the improvised mount for a searchlight on the vehicle in the foreground. There were five pintle mounts for machine guns around the inside perimeter of the vehicle's parapet. Pictorial evidence seems to indicate that no gun-shields were employed on the XM706E2 during the Vietnam War. (US Air Force Museum)

In this post-Vietnam War photograph is a US Air Force Security Forces XM706E2 fitted with gun shields. Both the M706 and the XM706E2 were powered by an engine that generated 191hp and provided a maximum speed on level roads of 60mph. They could cross a trench 1.5 feet wide and climb a vertical wall 24 inches high. (DOD)

During the post-Vietnam War era, the US Army had a small number of its surplus M706s pulled out of storage and modified to mimic externally and electronically two specific Soviet Army air-defence vehicles during aircraft and helicopter trials. The two modified M706s pictured were intended to represent the SA-9 Gaskin based on the 4 × 4 BRDM-2 series of armoured reconnaissance cars. (DOD)

Two US Army M706s modified to mimic externally and electronically a Soviet Army air-defence command and control vehicle based on the 4 × 4 BRDM-2 series of armoured reconnaissance cars. The standard M706 was 18.7 feet in length, 7.4 feet wide and 8 feet in height. Operational range of the vehicle on roads was between 425 and 600 miles. (DOD)

(*Opposite above*) The earliest improvised gun trucks employed by the US Army during the Vietnam War used sandbags enclosed in wooden frameworks to protect the machine-gunners located in the rear cargo bay of the vehicles. The follow-on gun trucks seen here were provided with armour kits designed and built in the United States. Notice however, the front windshields of the vehicles pictured are unarmoured. (*NA*)

(*Opposite below*) The machine-gunners in the rear cargo bay of the US Army gun truck pictured during the Vietnam War were protected by a locally produced open-topped armoured box. This sometimes proved an advantage in combat: when the gun trucks were struck and penetrated by enemy anti-tank rockets, a great deal of their explosive energy would be vented upwards. (*NA*)

(*Above*) A small number of military vehicle enthusiasts have taken upon themselves to create reproductions of the Vietnam War era US Army gun trucks, as seen here at a public air show in the United States. This particular example was built upon a 2.5-ton M35 Truck, which was built for the American military between 1950 and 1988, in three different versions. (*Loren Hannah*)

(*Opposite above*) Another type of gun truck that appeared during the Vietnam War involved the mounting of the power-operated Multiple Machine Gun Carriage M55 in the cargo bay of 2.5-ton or 5-ton cargo trucks, as seen in this Vietnam War era photograph. This type of gun truck was employed to guard the perimeter of US Army bases and convoys. (*NA*)

(*Above*) A modern-day reproduction of a Vietnam War era gun truck armed with the Multiple Machine Gun Carriage M55 in the cargo bay of a 5-ton truck. The powered gun mount first appeared during the Second World War and was typically seen mounted on specialized armoured halftracks such as the M16 Multiple Gun Motor Carriage. (*Loren Hannah*)

(*Opposite below*) The XM808 seen here was an 8 × 8 articulated AFV armed with a 20mm automatic cannon built for the US Army by the Lockheed Missile and Space Division Company. The company's name for the vehicle was the 'Twister'. Only the single example of the XM808 pictured was delivered for testing in 1970. It never went into production. (*TACOM*)

A novel design feature of the XM808 Twister was the fact that it had two engines; one in the forward body and the other in the rear body located behind the three-man crew compartment. Each engine produced 440hp. The vehicle was amphibious without prior preparation and could attain a water speed of 6mph. (*TACOM*)

One of two contenders for the US Army's early 1970s Armored Reconnaissance Scout Vehicle (ARSV) programme was the Lockheed Missile and Space Division Company's 6 × 6 submission seen here. The vehicle was designated as the XM800W, and as with the XM808 Twister, the XM800W was articulated, as is clearly evident in this picture. (*TACOM*)

Supposedly only the US Navy acquired a small number of Dragoon 300 4 × 4 AFVs to guard its nuclear weapon storage areas in the early 1980s. But at least one example of the vehicle came into US Army hands, as seen here during a training exercise in Egypt. The turret is fitted with an optical telescope that would transmit its picture via a data link to a higher headquarters. (*DOD*)

(*Opposite above*) Pictured in US Air Force service is the Cadillac Gage 4 × 4 armoured truck, referred to by the company as the 'Commando Ranger'. In US Air Force Service it was named the 'Peacekeeper'. A far less capable vehicle than the 4 × 4 XM706E2 it replaced as a base security vehicle in both armament and off-road capabilities, it was chosen for its low cost. (*DOD*)

(*Opposite below*) US Air Force security policemen during a training exercise with their Peacekeeper. The vehicle weighed 10,800lbs. Armor on the vehicle was listed as being able to protect it against 7.62mm ball ammunition. It had a length of 16.5 feet, a width of 8.7 feet, and a height of 7.4 feet. Listed maximum speed of the Peacekeeper was 70mph. (*DOD*)

(*Above*) The pilot model of the LAV-25 can be identified by the vision block on the side of the turret. There was a matching vision block on the other side of the turret. Both disappeared on the production units of the LAV-25. The camouflage paint scheme on the vehicle was developed by the US Army in the early 1970s and discontinued in the late 1980s. (*General Motors of Canada*)

(*Above*) The most important design features demanded by the American military for the eventual winner of the LAV programme competition was vehicle size and weight. All had to be readily transported by existing US Air Force transport planes. The USMC also wanted a vehicle that could be transported by the existing heavy lift helicopters, as seen here with an LAV-25 carried as a sling load. (*General Motors of Canada*)

(*Opposite above*) An important design feature of the LAV-25 was its ability to swim. Propulsion in the water for the vehicle is achieved with two propellers, one located on either side of the lower rear hull. In this picture we can see one of the two propellers of an LAV-25. The vehicle can only operate in calm inland water. (*DOD*)

(*Opposite below*) The maximum speed of the LAV-25 when in the water is 6.5mph. To provide stability for the vehicle when in the water, a large trim vane located under the front lower hull is erected manually by the crew. Upon exiting the water, the vehicle's driver can drop the trim vane from inside the vehicle and disengage its two propellers. (*Michael Green*)

(*Above*) The main armament of the LAV-25 seen here is its 25mm automatic cannon. To allow for the accurate fire of the automatic cannon on the LAV-25, it is equipped with a seven-power thermal day/night sight that provides the vehicle commander and gunner with the ability to see potential targets at a range of 4,400 yards. (*General Motors of Canada*)

(*Opposite above*) The 25mm automatic cannon mounted in the turret of the LAV-25 pictured is an electric-motor driven weapon with a maximum range of 3,000 yards. Notice on this vehicle that the propeller on the right side of the vehicle has been removed, no doubt so it and its counterpart on the other side of the vehicle would not be damaged during training exercises. (*Michael Green*)

(*Opposite below*) From an LAV-25 manual comes this illustration of the various components of the vehicle's turret. The 25mm automatic cannon mounted in the vehicle can destroy lightly-armoured vehicles, as well as slow and low-flying helicopters or aircraft. The vehicle commander of the LAV-25 has seven periscopes arrayed around his cupola. (*DOD*)

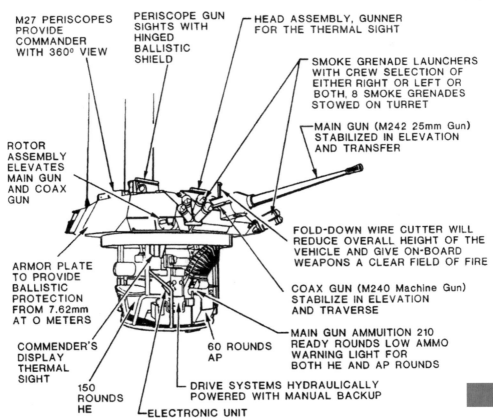

M27 PERISCOPES PROVIDE COMMANDER WITH 360° VIEW

PERISCOPE GUN SIGHTS WITH HINGED BALLISTIC SHIELD

HEAD ASSEMBLY, GUNNER FOR THE THERMAL SIGHT

SMOKE GRENADE LAUNCHERS WITH CREW SELECTION OF EITHER RIGHT OR LEFT OR BOTH, 8 SMOKE GRENADES STOWED ON TURRET

MAIN GUN (M242 25mm GUN) STABILIZED IN ELEVATION AND TRANSFER

ROTOR ASSEMBLY ELEVATES MAIN GUN AND COAX GUN

FOLD-DOWN WIRE CUTTER WILL REDUCE OVERALL HEIGHT OF THE VEHICLE AND GIVE ON-BOARD WEAPONS A CLEAR FIELD OF FIRE

ARMOR PLATE TO PROVIDE BALLISTIC PROTECTION FROM 7.62mm AT O METERS

COAX GUN (M240 Machine Gun) STABILIZE IN ELEVATION AND TRAVERSE

COMMENDER'S DISPLAY THERMAL SIGHT

60 ROUNDS AP

MAIN GUN AMMUITION 210 READY ROUNDS LOW AMMO WARNING LIGHT FOR BOTH HE AND AP ROUNDS

150 ROUNDS HE

DRIVE SYSTEMS HYDRAULICALLY POWERED WITH MANUAL BACKUP

ELECTRONIC UNIT THERMAL SIGHT

(*Above*) The USMC does not employ the LAV-25 as an armoured personnel carrier because it lacks an adequate amount of armour protection and passenger room to perform that role. Rather, the USMC uses it as a reconnaissance vehicle. As such, it normally carries four scouts in its rear hull compartment. In this picture we see the scouts of an LAV-25 dismounting during Operation Urgent Fury in 1983. (*DOD*)

(*Opposite above*) An LAV-25 on patrol in Panama during Operation Urgent Fury in 1983. The vehicle has a three-man crew: a vehicle commander and gunner who sit side-by-side in the power-operated turret, and a driver who sits in the left front hull alongside the engine. The engine on the LAV-25 produces 275hp, giving the vehicle a maximum road speed of 62mph. (*DOD*)

(*Opposite below*) Marines performing maintenance on their LAV-25s following Operation Urgent Fury in 1983. Visible in this picture are the open engine access hatches, as well as the open emergency hatch located on the left side of the upper hull. Also in this image are the driver's three periscopes. For night operations the center periscope can be replaced with a passive image intensifier. (*DOD*)

(*Opposite above*) Several LAV-25s during Operation Desert Shield in 1991, the prelude to Operation Desert Storm which occurred the same year. The vehicle weighs 28,100lbs, has a length of 21 feet, a width of 8 feet 2 inches and a height of 8 feet 4 inches. Secondary armament on the LAV-25 consists of two small-calibre machine guns; one of which is seen in this photograph. (*DOD*)

(*Opposite below*) An LAV-25 during Operation Iraqi Freedom in 2003. The 25mm main gun on the vehicle is the same as mounted in the US Army's series of M2/M3 series Bradley Infantry and Cavalry Fighting Vehicles. The LAV-25 has authorized storage space for 630 rounds of 25mm ammunition and 1,600 rounds of small-calibre ammunition for its two machine guns. (*DOD*)

(*Above*) Because the LAV-25 has no way of defending itself from tanks, every Light Armored Reconnaissance Battalion (LAR) in the USMC (equipped with sixty LAV-25s) has sixteen units of the LAV-AT, one of which is shown here. It has a power-operated turret, seen in its stowed position, that contains two TOW-2 missile launchers and the gunner's sighting equipment. (*General Motors of Canada*)

The various components that make up the power-operated turret on the LAV-AT in this illustration from a manual. The builders of the anti-tank missile armed turret on the vehicle refer to it as the TOW Under-Armor (TUA) turret. When erected, the TUA extends 5 feet above the vehicle's hull and can be rotated 360 degrees. (*DOD*)

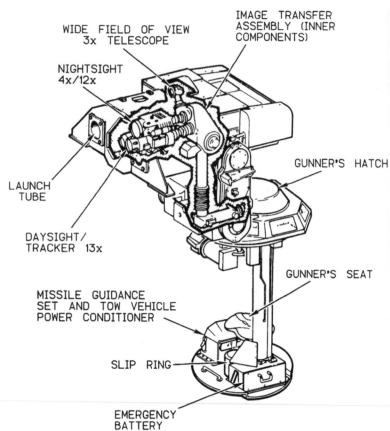

IMAGE TRANSFER ASSEMBLY (INNER COMPONENTS)

WIDE FIELD OF VIEW 3x TELESCOPE

NIGHTSIGHT 4x/12x

GUNNER'S HATCH

LAUNCH TUBE

DAYSIGHT/ TRACKER 13x

GUNNER'S SEAT

MISSILE GUIDANCE SET AND TOW VEHICLE POWER CONDITIONER

SLIP RING

EMERGENCY BATTERY

Shown at the moment of firing is a TOW anti-tank missile exiting the TUA turret of an LAV-AT. The sighting equipment on the TUA consists of a 12-power day/night thermal sight that can engage enemy tanks during periods of reduced visibility. The TUA is popularly referred to by its unofficial nickname as the 'Hammerhead'. It is raised and lowered by a hydraulic trunnion assembly. (*DOD*)

The crew of the LAV-AT, with its TUA in the lowered stored position, consists of four individuals: the vehicle commander, the driver, the gunner located in the one-man compartment of the TUA, and the loader who resides in the rear hull compartment. Besides the two anti-tank missiles in the launcher unit, the rear hull compartment had storage room for an additional fourteen. *(Michael Green)*

To keep the LAV-AT a viable weapon system for the future it is being fitted with a new power-operated anti-tank missile armed turret as seen on the vehicle pictured. It is referred to as the Anti-tank Weapon System (ATWS) turret. It includes new advanced thermal sighting and guidance control systems. Unlike the older-generation TUA, the ATWS allows for the firing of anti-tank missiles while the vehicle is moving. *(DOD)*

(*Above*) A picture of the LAV-M variant shows the closed three-section hatch on the roof of the vehicle. When shut it protects the vehicle's mortar crew from enemy artillery and mortar airbursts, as well as from the elements. The thin vertical metal stock in front of the driver's position cuts any wires or cables strung across the vehicle's path. (*General Motors of Canada*)

(*Opposite above*) Line illustration from a manual showing the interior layout of the LAV-M. The 81mm dismountable mortar rests on a 360-degree rotating turntable located in the rear hull compartment of the vehicle. There is space in the LAV-M for ninety rounds of 81mm ammunition. The normal mix is sixty-eight high-explosive (HE) rounds, nine smoke rounds and thirteen illuminating rounds. (*DOD*)

(*Opposite below*) The photographer managed to catch the moment of firing from an LAV-M's 81mm mortar. The crew of the vehicle includes five men: driver, vehicle commander and a three-man mortar crew. The entrance or egress for the mortar crew is through two large doors at the rear of the LAV-M, which is also found on most of the other LAV-series vehicles. (*DOD*)

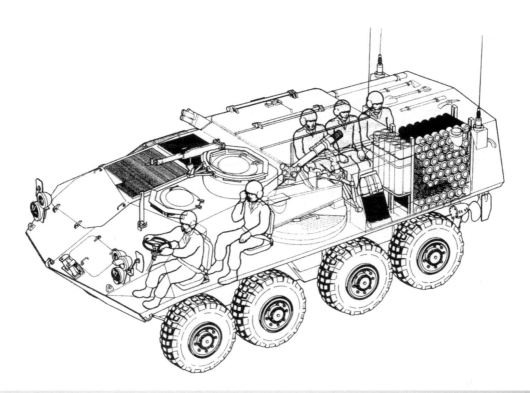

(*Above*) The original configuration of the FMC candidate vehicle the firm submitted to the USMC for its LAV-AD competition in 1990. The turret was armed with a 25mm automatic cannon, a single quadruple launcher for surface-to-air missiles and twin seven-tube rocket launching pods. Testing revealed that the rockets were ineffective in the ground-to-air role and they were replaced with another quadruple launcher for surface-to-air missiles. (*FMC*)

(*Opposite above*) The winning contender for the USMC requirement for an LAV-AD variant was the vehicle shown here submitted by General Electric. It was armed with a 25mm Gatling-type automatic cannon and two quadruple launchers for surface-to-air missiles. There is storage room in the rear hull compartment of the GE LAV-AD for an additional eight surface-to-air missiles. (*General Electric*)

(*Opposite below*) For the logistical version of the LAV series labelled the LAV-L, the rear hull compartment roof was raised, as is evident in this picture. Cargo can be inserted or removed from the vehicle through two large overlapping doors at the rear of the vehicle or via a two-piece folding overhead hatch. The vehicle commander's cupola is located directly behind the driver's position on a slightly raised platform, visible here. (*DOD*)

(*Opposite above*) This LAV-R is fitted with a rotating hydraulic crane capable of lifting a 6,000lbs maximum load and a rear-mounted winch with a maximum pull capacity of 30,000lbs. The vehicle's crew consists of three men: driver, vehicle commander and rigger. A welding generator and associated equipment is carried inside the rear hull compartment. (*DOD*)

(*Above*) Looking very much like the LAV-L is this variant labelled as the LAV-C2 (Battalion Command and Control Vehicle). Like the LAV-L, the rear hull compartment has been raised. Unlike the LAV-L, the LAV-C2 has two cupolas: one directly behind the driver for the vehicle commander and the second for the battalion commander on the forward portion of the raised rear hull compartment. (*General Motors of Canada*)

(*Opposite below*) An LAV-C2 in Afghanistan with a number of wartime additions. These include the two large vertical antennas at the front of the vehicle intended to jam radio signals between insurgent transmitters and the improvised explosive devices (IEDs) they deploy on roadsides to attack the vehicles. In addition, notice the storage brackets for carrying extra rations. (*DOD*)

(*Above*) Seen in this builder's marketing photo is the original configuration of the Mobile Electronic Warfare Support System (MEWSS) vehicle of the LAV series. It looks very similar to the LAV-L and the LAV-C2 variants with the raised rear hull compartment. The obvious difference is the large horizontal-oriented antenna array. (*General Motors of Canada*)

(*Opposite above*) The current configuration of the Mobile Electronic Warfare Support System (MEWSS) version of the LAV series. The large horizontal antenna array seen on the vehicle when initially introduced into service between 1987 and 1989 is gone. It was replaced by the telescopic mast seen behind the vehicle commander cupola in its stored position. (*Michael Green*)

(*Opposite below*) On a training exercise in Norway is the improved A2 version of the LAV-25. Unlike the A1 version of the vehicle that had no external identifying features that would distinguish it from the original production vehicles, new-built LAV-25A2s, as well as LAV-25A1s upgraded to the A2 standard, have an add-on armour kit affixed to both the turret and the hull. Those portions of the add-on armour kit affixed to the hull are identified by the rounded studs visible in this photograph. (*DOD*)

(*Above*) The biggest threat to the LAV series serving in war zones were improvised explosive devices (IEDs) and later explosively formed penetrators (EFPs). To address these weapons, the USMC sought out additional protection for the vehicle commanders and gunners of the LAV-25 from roadside shrapnel when exposed. This was done by providing them with the dismountable armoured parapets seen here, which are fitted with vision blocks. (*DOD*)

(*Opposite above*) In this picture of the rear hull compartment of an LAV-25A2 we can see the hull vision blocks for the four scouts normally carried on the vehicle, although there is enough room for six in this area. Visible at the far end of the compartment is the gunner's control panel and the bottom portion of the turret basket behind the metal safety barrier. (*Chris Hughes*)

(*Opposite below*) Coming off a US Navy landing craft is an LAV-25A2. All the various models of the LAV-A2 series have been fitted with numerous expandable hull storage brackets as visible in this photo. To offset the weight gains imposed by the various armour kits applied to the LAV-A2 series, a number of suspension upgrades were made to the design. (*DOD*)

(*Above*) Taking part in a training exercise are two LAVs, with the one in the foreground being an LAV-25A2 and the vehicle behind it an LAV-LA2. A key upgrade made to the LAV-25A2 was in its fire-control system. While the main armament of the vehicle remains the same, the addition of a new more advanced fire-control system, including a laser finder, means the combat effectiveness of the vehicle has dramatically improved. (*DOD*)

(*Opposite above*) Shown at the moment of firing is an LAV-25A2. The dual-fed weapon system on the 25mm automatic cannon is externally powered by a 1.5hp direct current (DC) motor, which allows it three different firing rates. These include single shot, a low rate of 100 rounds per minute (plus or minus 25 rounds per minute) and a high rate of 200 rounds per minute (plus or minus 25 rounds per minute). (*DOD*)

(*Opposite below*) A crewman of an LAV-25A2 preparing to load 25mm ammunition into his vehicle. The 25mm automatic cannon on the vehicle can fire five different rounds of ammunition. For dealing with lightly armoured enemy vehicles, such as armoured scout cars and armoured personnel carriers, it uses the M971 Armor-Piercing Discarding Sabot with Tracer (APDS-T). (*DOD*)

(*Opposite above*) The job of the US Army's M93A1 Fox NBC-RS (Nuclear Biological Chemical, Reconnaissance System) is to locate, identify and mark contaminated areas of a battlefield. The vehicle has an onboard radiation monitor and a small sampling wheel that picks up soil to test for contaminants. It is equipped with an over-pressure filtration system to protect the crew from airborne contaminants. (*DOD*)

(*Opposite below*) This M93A1 Fox NBC-RS is powered by a 320hp engine that provides it a maximum road speed of 62mph. It is amphibious and its two propellers (one of which is visible at the bottom rear hull) can propel it through calm inland waterways at up to 6mph. The vehicle is 22.2 feet long, with a width of 9.9 feet and a height of 8.1 feet. The vehicle has a crew of four men. (*DOD*)

(*Above*) The latest version of the M93 Fox NBC-RS series designated as the M93A1P1. It is equipped with an enhanced NBC detection system, seen in its raised position projecting out of a roof hatch. The new NBC detection system automatically alerts all other vehicles connected to the same Global Positioning System (GPS) to an identified NBC threat and its location. (*GDLS*)

Chapter Four

The High Mobility Multipurpose Wheeled Vehicle

In the early 1980s, the American military took into service the 4 × 4 High Mobility Multipurpose Wheeled Vehicle (HMMWV) designed and built by the AM General Corporation. The HMMWV was originally named the 'Hummer' by the builder, later replaced by the name 'Humvee'. Both names are registered trademarks of AM General. The Hummer name was later used by AM General for its civilian models of the vehicle.

The HMMWV was the replacement for a number of vehicles, including the 4 × 4 M151 MUTT (Military Unit Tactical Truck) series, the 6 × 6 M561 Gamma Goat and the 4 × 4 Commercial Utility Cargo Trucks (CUCVs). The latter, while more affordable than specialized military trucks, lacked the durability the services sought.

The bulk of the HMMWVs ordered for the American military were non-armoured, weaponless transport trucks. A smaller number were referred to as armament carriers, and could be fitted with a variety of weapons ranging from machine guns to an anti-tank missile launcher known as the TOW (tube-launched optically-tracked wire-guided).

HMMWV Designations

Those armament carriers in US Army and US Air Force service that were armed with a machine gun or grenade launcher were referred to as the M1025, and when fitted with a winch they became the M1026. US Army armament carriers fitted with the TOW were labelled as the M966. Those with TOW and fitted with a winch were referred to as the M1036.

Armament carriers taken into service by the US Army and US Air Force had bullet-resistant windows and doors, which were intended to stop small bullet fragments. This armour arrangement is referred to as 'basic armour' and can be identified by an X-shaped stamping on the four doors of US Army and US Air Force armament carriers.

Armament carriers acquired by the USMC came with an armour arrangement referred to as 'supplemental armour'. It consisted of flat steel armour plates attached to various portions of the vehicles, including over the existing basic armour X-shaped stamped doors. The supplemental armour add-on kit provided protection from larger bullet fragments than the basic armour kit.

Due to their supplemental armour kit, USMC armament carriers were assigned different designations than the same vehicle employed by the other services. Those fitted with either a machine gun or grenade launcher where labelled the M1043, while the same vehicle with a winch became the M1044. The TOW armament carrier employed by the USMC without a winch was designated the M1045, and with a winch as the M1046.

AM General tried to anticipate future US Army requirements in 1991 and, using their newest version of the HMMWV, referred to as the M1097 Heavy Humvee Variant (HHV), they created an up-armoured armament carrier. It was not ordered by the US Army, although some were sold to friendly foreign governments.

A large number of US Army and USMC HMMWV armament carriers participated in the ground war portion of Operation Desert Storm in 1991. However, such was the brevity of that land-based conflict that little or no insight was gained on their combat utility, or lack thereof.

New Types of Conflicts

In 1993, US Army units were deployed to Somalia in support of United Nations peacekeeping duties. In a country in which almost every male citizen was armed with a high-powered assault rifle, it was soon clear to the US Army that the limited armour protection found on its various versions of the HMMWV armament carrier (protected by the basic armour kit) left its soldiers highly vulnerable.

In a quick-fix approach, the US Army had AM General team up with the O'Gara-Hess & Eisenhardt Armoring Company, a long-time builder of armoured vehicles for the commercial market. They took an M1097 HHV Shelter Carrier chassis and armoured it to new US Army specifications. This mating produced the XM1109 Up-Armored HMMWV (UAH) in 1993. After a brief test period, the vehicle was standardized by the US Army in 1994 as the M1109 UAH.

The Next Round Vehicle

Positive results with the M1109 UAH resulted in the US Army going back to AM General and the O'Gara-Hess & Eisenhardt Armoring Company and asking for an improved version based on the newest model of the HMMWV being built. That vehicle was named the Expanded Capacity Humvee (ECH) by AM General. Employing the ECH baseline chassis, the two firms came up with the XM1114 UAH for field testing in 1995.

In an article by First Lieutenant Jonathan C. Byrom that appeared in the January–February 1998 issue of *Armor* magazine titled 'Up-armored HMMWVs: Answer for

Peacekeeping Operations', he describes the usefulness of the XM1114 UAH during operations in Bosnia-Herzegovina, located in the Balkans:

> The XM1114 uses significantly less fuel than both [M2/M3] Bradleys and M1A1 [Abrams] tanks. My platoon was able to patrol for an entire day and use less than 30 gallons of fuel per vehicle compared to the hundreds of gallons needed by Bradleys and tanks during the same patrol duration ... Another strength of the up-armoured Humvee is its mobility. It can traverse some terrain that a tank or Bradley cannot, particularly tight spaces in villages and wooded terrain ... The XM1114 equipped platoon is also effective because it preserves the roads, unlike tracked vehicles ... The XM1114 HMMWV is also equipped with combat locks on each door, which allows it to function effectively in the riot situations that soldiers often encounter in tense peacekeeping or peace-enforcing operations.

The XM1114 UAH entered into series production for the US Army in 1996 as the M1114 UAH. The US Air Force (USAF) was impressed enough with the new M1114 UAH for it to order a modified version, designated the M1116 UAH; it entered into the USAF inventory in 1998. The USAF also employs an unarmed version of the M1114 UAH, designated as the M1145 UAH, for its forward air controllers (FACs).

HMMWV Designation Changes

In 1994, the US Army began receiving the newest model of the HMMWV referred to as the A1 series, all of which were based on the Heavy Hummer Variant (HHV) chassis. At that point, all the initial series production models of the HMMWV were assigned the A0 suffix to their original vehicle designation codes. For example, the M966 TOW missile carrier without a winch, and fitted with the basic armor kit, became the M966A0.

With the introduction of the A2 series model of the HMMWV in 1995, the US Army did away with the separate designation for those armament carriers with basic armor and equipped with winches, and those fitted with TOW. The only armament carrier designation for the US Army became the M1025A2 and the M1121A2 armament/TOW carrier with basic armor.

The USMC decided that its version of the armament/TOW carrier with the supplemental armor kit would retain not only a separate designation, but would also retain different designations for those fitted with and without winches. This resulted in the M1043A2 armament/TOW carrier and the M1045A2 armament/TOW carrier with the supplemental armor kit.

HMMWVs and Asymmetric Warfare

In response to a Taliban Insurgency that began in 2003, a large number of US Army and USMC combat units deployed to Afghanistan, all of which brought their various models of the HMMWVs, both armoured and non-armoured. US Army Special Forces member Eric Evans relates a story about his M1114 UAH encountering a large IED in Afghanistan in January 2003:

> The explosion that hit us picked our vehicle up and tossed it more than 10 feet in the air. My teammates found pieces of the vehicle more than 150 metres away from the explosion. I ended up at the hospital and received 48 stitches and 9 staples in my head, and the driver ended up with a few stitches in his leg and a nice cut on his head. Amazingly, we all walked away … I then saw the vehicle [his unrepaired M1114 UAH] at the Association of the United States Army conference in Washington DC, and it was awe-inspiring to see how much damage the explosion had done to my vehicle, yet how little damage was done to the interior of the vehicle.

In an interview conducted in Afghanistan in June 2004 by a Marine Corps public affairs member with Marines from the 22nd Marines Expeditionary Unit (Special Operations Capable), every Marine present stated that the one vehicle that had been involved in every operation since they had arrived in the country in April 2004, from vehicular reconnaissance patrols to combat offensives, was an M1114 UAH, affectionately nicknamed 'Alone and Unafraid'.

A New Theatre of Operation

As the US Army planned for its part in Operation Iraqi Freedom in early 2003, it could not envision any requirement for the M1114 UAH. The unforeseen Iraqi Insurgency that began in the summer of 2003 resulted in a quick change of opinion about the usefulness of the vehicle. By April of the following year, there were approximately 2,500 units of the M1114 UAH in Iraq.

To fulfill the demand in Iraq for even more M1114 UAHs, the US Army placed a rush order in April 2004 for an additional 2,000 units of the vehicle. All were delivered before the end of 2004. Yet there were still not enough of them to meet the needs of the soldiers in Iraq. It was envisioned by the US Army in 2004 that it would need at least 8,000 units of the M1114 UAH to deal with the rising tempo of the insurgency.

In a 2004 US Army public affairs article, Gary Motsek, deputy director of Support Operations for the US Army Material Command, stated that the requirement for 8,000 M1114 UAHs in Iraq was once considered unthinkable. However, because it was easier to manoeuvre in some of the tight urban spaces within Iraq, the M1114 UAH became by default, in Motsek's words, 'the platform of choice'. Motsek went on to say, 'If anybody would have told me a Humvee would be the platform of choice in war, I would have told them they're crazy.' By 2007, there were approximately 20,000 UAH in service overseas with the American military.

The M1114 UAH was a big improvement over early HMMWV armament carriers, but despite all the extra armour added to the vehicles, there were limits to what it could protect against, as there are with all AFVs. In early March 2005, General Michael Hagee, then commandant of the USMC, told reporters a fully armoured HMMWV had been, as he described it, 'ripped apart, just torn apart' by an Iraqi insurgent IED consisting of three 155mm artillery shells linked together to go off all at the same time.

Brigadier General William Cato of Marine Corps Systems Command described the evolving threats in Iraq to a Congressional House Armed Services Meeting in May 2005: 'Insurgent IED threats once chiefly consisted of 60mm, 81mm mortar kinds of rounds.' He then pointed out that the insurgents had begun using 122mm and 155mm artillery shells, as well as 500-pound bombs and double-stacked anti-tank mines to provide more explosive power for their IEDs. 'As we've added armour they've added greater explosives,' Cato told the Congressmen.

Armoring Early-Model HMMWVs

When the US Army ordered the non-armoured cargo/troop carrier models of the HMMWV in the early 1980s, they were considered rear-area non-combat vehicles. However, with the Iraqi Insurgency it soon became apparent that there were no non-combat rear areas, as is typical for asymmetric warfare. All American military vehicles and personnel were considered targets of opportunity by the Iraqi insurgents wherever they might be found.

Like the Vietnam War, the soldiers and the Marines on the ground in Iraq quickly developed a wide variety of improvised add-on armour kits for all of their non-armoured wheeled vehicles, especially the HMMWV as it was one of the most common wheeled vehicles in Iraq in 2003. An impression of these improvised armour kits, sometimes nicknamed 'Hillbilly Armor' due to their make-shift appearance, comes from US Army Captain Jerry Diamond:

> The quality of design and construction varies very dramatically, from fairly well manufactured to rolling death traps. As a rule, most of the steel is local carbon steel, about 4mm thick. It offers little protection from anything short of a thrown rock. Worse, when struck by a high-velocity round, not only will the round penetrate the thin steel plates, the steel itself will spall [break up into small fragments], adding to the danger for the soldiers inside the vehicles.

The US Army Research Development and Engineering Command (RDECOM) soon came up with its own version of an add-on armour kit for all the various HMMWVs, including armament carriers. They would refer to it as the Armor Survivability Kit (ASK), the first example of which showed up in Iraq in October 2003.

Major Dan Rusin, leader of the ASK team at Aberdeen Proving Ground, talked about the construction of the up-armour package in a US Army Public Affairs released article in 2004: 'We tried an assortment of products from aluminum composites, a lot of fancy stuff. But we came back to the same armoured steel that you make tanks from.'

The downside of encasing the two-door and four-door unarmoured HMMWVs in the ASK was heat build-up, which soon became a serious issue in Iraq; it was solved by adding Red-Dot air-conditioning units to the vehicles.

In addition to its own in-house ASK, the US Army contracted with Armor Holdings, which had acquired the O'Gara-Hess & Eisenhardt Armoring Company in 1996, to provide an add-on armour kit for some versions of the unarmoured HMMWV cargo/troop carriers. The company referred to their product as the 'lightweight HMMWV armoured demountable (HArD) kit'. It provided a superior level of protection than that offered by the US Army's in-house developed ASK.

USMC Respond to the Threat

The HArD kit was also ordered by the USMC in late 2003 for some versions of its unarmoured HMMWV cargo/troop carriers. In addition, Armor Holdings added, at the service's request, new ballistic windshields for their vehicles. Despite the addition of the HArD kits, it was not uncommon for Marines to add additional improvised armour to their vehicles.

In 2005, the USMC began the fielding of a new in-house developed add-on armour kit they named the Marine Armor Kit (MAK). The MAK started as a collaborative effort between the USMC and US Army, but the latter dropped out of the programme.

Unlike the HArD kits, the MAK was adaptable to all the various versions of the HMMWV. Major James Washburn, a Marine Corps System Command project officer who worked on the MAK programme describes the difficulties of developing it:

> It's a huge task to match armour protection against the evolving threat while staying within the carrying capacity of the wheeled vehicle fleet. You simply can't retrofit a HMMWV to match the armour protection of a main battle tank. Our main objective is to make sure the Marines get the best possible protection in the time frame they need it.

Like the US Army's in-house ASK, the MAK, when applied to the USMC HMMWV fleet in Iraq, created a serious problem for the crews with heat build-up inside their vehicles. This resulted in the quick addition of air-conditioning units to all HMMWVs that had the MAK.

The M1114 UAH in USMC Service

Besides the HArD kits and their in-house MAK programme, the USMC had showed no interest in the M1114 UAH prior to the Iraqi Insurgency. Its outbreak pushed the senior leadership of the USMC to change their mind, and in 2004 they ordered 498 units of the vehicle from AM General. They were also provided additional M1114 UAHs from the US Army inventory and M1116 UAHs from the US Air Force inventory.

In a June 2004 interview conducted by USMC public affairs in Iraq, Gunnery Sergeant Paul L. Jones, a motor transportation chief with the 2nd Battalion, 4th Marine Regiment, stated the following: 'Right now the battalion has seventeen M1116 up-armoured Humvees and ten M1114 heavy variant Humvees.' His shop chief, Sergeant Jay C. Asland, stated that they had been very pleased with the performance of both types of Humvees: 'These things are covered in armour. The doors, the under panels, and the side panels all are protected by thick steel.' Asland went on to say: 'The windows are made of glass that's almost four inches thick.'

One of the most popular features the Marines found with being issued the M1114 or M1116 UAHs was their built-in air-conditioning. The biggest drawback to the new vehicles appears in a quote by Lance Corporal Philip E. Truman, who stated: 'With all the communications equipment and the AC [air-conditioning] unit that take up so much space, they're not very comfortable to ride in.' While the ride might not be much fun in an M1151 or M1116 UAH, Truman went on to comment: 'I'd rather be safer than comfortable.'

FRAG Kits

With the insurgents in both Iraq and Afghanistan constantly improving upon their anti-vehicle weapons, the US Army developed another quick-fix approach to better protecting their fleet of M1114 UAHs: Fragmentation Armor Field Kits (FRAGs).

The initial FRAG was labelled 1A. It was followed by FRAGs two through four. All were developed to counter under-vehicle explosions. None of them were easily identifiable on the M1114 UAH without close inspection – not until the advent of the interim FRAG 5 and then the standard FRAG 5, both of which can be identified by a set of thickly armoured doors.

The Newest UAH HMMWV

Combat experience gained with the M1114 UAH during the early part of the Iraqi and Afghanistan Insurgencies was incorporated into a next generation HMMWV armament carrier designated the M1151 UAH. It entered into series production in 2005 and is based on the chassis of the newest version of the HMMWV built by AM General. It is known as the Reliability Enhanced M1100 Series HMMWV.

A sub-variant of the M1151 UAH is designated the M1167 TOW ITAS Carrier. Both were later upgraded to an A1 standard in 2009.

The factory-installed armour packages fitted to the M1114 UAHs were not capable of accepting add-on armour kits. The Reliability Enhanced M1100 Series M1151 and M1167 UAHs were originally designed to be fitted with mounting hardware able to accept various add-on armour kits. The American military refers to this as an 'armour capable' vehicle. Add-on armour kits are also classified by the American military as 'scalable armour'.

The US Army eventually decided that it preferred the M1151 and M1167 series UAHs to come off the production line with a factory affixed base armour package, which AM General labels as the A Kit. It was designed to accept an additional add-on armour kit that AM General refers to as a B1 Kit.

According to AM General marketing literature, the B1 Kit can be either factory installed or field installed, and when combined with the A Kit provides both under-body mine and upper-body ballistic protection to the M1151A1 series UAHs. If the threat level decreases, the B1 Kit can be removed from the vehicles. There is also a B3 kit for the M1151A1 series UAHs consisting of perimeter armour, overhead armour and a rear ballistic bulkhead.

Other vehicles based on the Reliability Enhanced M1100 Series HMMWV include the M1165/M1165A1 and the M1152/M1152A1. The four-door M1165/M1165A1 is a command and control vehicle and the M1152/M1152A1 a multi-purpose platform that can be configured as a troop carrier, cargo carrier, or shelter carrier. The A through to B3 Kits were also designed to be mountable on the M1165A1 and M1152A1 if required.

FRAG Kits for the M1151 Series

Besides the A through to B3 Kits developed for the M1151 series UAH, there were also two FRAGs developed that could be fitted to the M1151 and M1167 UAH series, as well as the older generation M1114 UAH. These were labelled FRAG 6 and 7.

FRAG 6 could be identified by extremely large external boxes fitted to a vehicle's doors. They were intended to protect the occupants of the vehicles from explosively formed penetrators (EFPs). However, it proved a failure in service because the external boxes did not prove durable enough in the field. Another problem was the extra width FRAG 6 added to the vehicles so fitted, thereby reducing their manoeuvrability in urban areas.

Due to the various design shortcomings of FRAG 6 it was replaced by FRAG 7 in 2009. The latter lacked the large boxes seen on the doors of vehicles fitted with FRAG 6. A key external identifying feature of those vehicles fitted with FRAG 7 was a removable overhead armour protection on existing OGP-K turrets. FRAG 7 overhead cover could not be installed on GPK turrets.

From a US Army public affairs article dated 9 April 2009 appears this extract regarding what the new turret design, which formed part of FRAG 7, brought to the M1114 and M1151 series UAHs:

FRAG 7 introduces the ARDEC [Armament Research, Development and Engineering Center] developed and Army Depot produced Overhead Cover (OHC), which provides the capability of the gunner to view the battlefield without compromising safety. Fitted with transparent glass, the OHC provides protection from the sun, while still allowing the gunner to maintain situational awareness.

In addition to the OHC, FRAG 7 also consisted of new more-durable tyres and wheel assemblies for the M1114 and M1151 series UAHs. Together these provided increased reliability compared to the tyre and wheel assemblies found on earlier models of the HMMWV series UAHs, which sometimes failed under hard usage.

The M1151 Series Problems

The addition of ever more armour to the HMMWV design, despite the continuous upgrades and improvement to the vehicle's chassis, has not been without problems, as can be found in a report issued by the US Army Program Manager: Light Tactical Vehicles, on 7 October 2011. In that report are a number of quotes from unnamed US Army soldiers on their impressions of the M1151A1 series UAHs:

1. The weight is too much for the engine. Engine parts are breaking because of the extra weight added.
2. The vehicle moves slower. The acceleration, ventilation and air conditioning is not good.
3. 'The vehicle lacks power. It would stall or lose all power (pedal to the floor) and the truck goes nowhere during missions.
4. The vehicle's acceleration is much worse and the brakes are not holding up. The vehicle is too heavy, and needs upgraded brakes.

Special Force Humvees

For use by American military Special Operation Forces (SOFs) there is an armoured version of the M1165A1 command and control vehicle referred to as Ground Mobility Vehicle (GMV). The builder labels it as the 'Special Operation HMMW2V'. As with the M1151A1 series UAHs, it came with the base A Kit and can be upgraded to the B1 or B3 Kit.

Depending on the user, the GMV has a number of slightly different designations. The US Navy SEAL variant is labelled as the GMV-Navy (GMV-N). Those employed by the US Army Rangers are referred to as the GMV-R, while those used by the US

Army Special Operations Command for its Special Operation Forces (SOF) go by the designation GMV-S SOF. The UMSC has a version designated the GMV-M.

The M1151 UAH Series Replacement

The US Army was well aware of the design shortcoming of the M1151 UAH series, as well as all the other variants that made up the aging HMMWV series. It had therefore long planned on acquiring a new series of 4 × 4 vehicles, which they went ahead and labelled as the Joint Light Tactical Vehicle (JLTV), the 'joint' in the title meaning that it is also intended for use by the other services, in particular the USMC.

Testing JLTV prototypes submitted by companies interested in winning a contract began in 2013. After extensive review, the US Army chose the JLTV submitted by the Oshkosh Corporation in August 2015. Plans call for the building of 55,000 units of the JLTV at an estimated cost of $30 billion. Production is scheduled to begin in 2018, with operational capability being attained the following year.

The JLTV series is comprised of two variants. A two-seat model referred to as the Combat Support Vehicle (CSV) is fitted with an armoured cab that has a rear platform able to accept a variety of loads, labelled 'mission packages' by the US military. The second is a four-seat weapon-armed model referred to as a Combat Tactical Vehicle (CTV). Both variants are able to be fitted with various up-armouring kits if required.

This prototype of the AM General Humvee armament carrier variant is armed with an automatic grenade launcher. External features that identify it as a prototype include the four windshield wipers and the horizontal engine grille work. Notice that AM General has stencilled the name 'Hummer' on the front bumper of the vehicle, a registered trademark of the firm. (*AM General*)

(*Above*) The vehicle pictured is the AM General prototype of their proposed Humvee TOW Missile Carrier variant. The engine grille work is now vertical, which is seen on all the different production versions of the HMMWV, both armoured and non-armoured. Not seen on this prototype are the three holes in the bumpers of production non-winch-equipped vehicles. (*AM General*)

(*Opposite above*) A photograph of a US Army M1025A0 Armament Carrier in Panama during Operation Urgent Fury in 1989, fitted with the basic armour package that can be identified by the X-shaped stampings on the doors. A key external spotting feature of all Humvee armament carriers is the thin armoured hatchback-like enclosure at the rear of the vehicle. (*DOD*)

(*Opposite below*) In this posed picture taken during Operation Desert Storm in 1991 is a US Army M966A0 TOW Missile Carrier. The 5 foot 6 inch long 50lb TOW anti-tank missile is stored within a disposable launch tube that is manually inserted into the launcher unit tube seen in this picture prior to firing. The gunner on the vehicle is aiming the anti-tank missile with a 13-power daylight telescopic sight. (*DOD*)

(*Above*) In this dramatically-composed company marketing photograph is an M1026A1 Armament Carrier armed with a small-calibre machine gun. Unlike the non-ballistic front windshields on the A0 series of non-armoured HMMWVs, their armoured counterparts had ballistic windshields that consisted of a 2-inch-thick polycarbonate material that could stop bullet fragments. (*AM General*)

(*Opposite above*) This picture taken during Operation Iraqi Freedom in 2003 shows a US Army M1025A1 Armament Carrier armed with a large-calibre machine gun. The A1 version of the HMMWV series was introduced into service with the American military in 1993, and the A2 version in 1995. The A2 models have a rear bumper added, which provides increased towing capacity. There were nineteen different variants of the A0 HMMWV series, thirteen with the A1 model and only nine with the A2 model. (*DOD*)

(*Opposite below*) The USMC desired a slightly higher level of protection from bullet fragments for its armoured HMMWVs than the US Army. Therefore the doors on their A0 through A2 armoured variants were fitted with additional thin armoured plates that covered the X-shaped stampings, as seen on this M1045 or M1046 TOW Missile Carrier. (*Michael Green*)

(*Above*) This overhead view of a USMC M1043A2 Armament/TOW Missile Carrier shows the vehicle's armament mounting kit featuring a 32-inch weapon ring with a pedestal mount and quick release cradle. This was the same armament mounting kit found on the A0 and A1 series of armoured HMMWVs employed by all the services. (*DOD*)

(*Opposite above*) Shown during a training exercise is an M1043A0 or M1043A1 Armament Carrier in the foreground armed with a large-calibre machine gun. The vertical engine air intake tube located at the left-hand front side of the vehicle, and the engine exhaust extension coming out of the rear bottom of the vehicle on the right side, form part of the vehicle's deep water fording kit and are only seen on USMC HMMWVs. (*Michael Green*)

(*Opposite below*) Based on the chassis of the discontinued M1035 Shelter Carrier without a winch is this USMC anti-aircraft version of the HMMWV named the 'Avenger'. Also employed by the US Army, the Avenger consists of a one-man, electrically powered turret armed with tow pods, each containing four heat-seeking surface-to-air missiles, and a large-calibre machine gun. (*Michael Green*)

(*Opposite above*) Racing into action is this M1045 or M1046 TOW Missile Carrier with its crew at the ready during Operation Iraqi Freedom in 2003. The HMMWV is approximately 15 feet long, 7 feet wide and 6 feet tall. With its supplemental armour kit, the A2 model of the USMC armament/TOW carrier weighs in at about 10,300lbs. Maximum speed is listed at 60mph. (*DOD*)

(*Opposite below*) The supplemental armour kit visible on this Humvee would mark it as belonging to the USMC at first glance. However, it lacks the deep water kit extensions seen on all USMC HMMWVs, making it a US Army M1025A2 Armament/TOW Missile Carrier. Where it acquired its supplemental armour kit is unknown. The strange-looking attachment fitted to the vehicle's large-calibre machine gun is a blank-firing adapter employed during a training exercise. (*Michael Green*)

(*Above*) The up-armoured M1097 HHV (Heavy Hummer Variant) pictured was a private developmental venture by AM General in the early 1990s but not adopted by the American military. It was based on the chassis of the unarmoured M1097 HHV Cargo/Troop Carrier introduced into American military service in 1992. The following year, the improved M1097A1 version was introduced. (*AM General*)

(*Opposite above*) A US Army M1114 UAH on patrol in Afghanistan. Protection for the machine-gunner is provided by the Gunner's Shield Kit (GSK). The M1114 UAH came about because the US Army believed that the M1109 UAH was overloaded. To resolve this issue, the US Army asked for a similarly armoured version built upon AM General's new more powerful M1113 ECH (Expanded Capacity Humvee). (*DOD*)

(*Opposite below*) The M1114 UAH armour package was intended to provide protection from 7.62mm armour-piercing ammunition fired from ranges in excess of 100 yards. An under-armour plate, located under the front tyres of the vehicle, was supposed to protect against a 12lb mine blast. Here we see an M1114 subjected to a mine blast of unknown size at the US Army testing facility. (*O'Gara-Hess & Eisenhardt*)

(*Above*) Taking part in a driver's training course is an M1114 UAH in the markings of the American-trained and equipped Iraqi Army. Prominent in this picture is the protruding engine grille, an identifying feature of all the HMMWV series vehicles, which are based on the chassis of the ECH (Expanded Capacity Humvee). The engine on the ECH series produces 190hp. (*DOD*)

(*Above*) On display at a museum is this near mint example of the M1114 UAH. Due to the high losses of machine-gunners on the M1114 UAHs fitted only with the forward-facing Gunner's Shield Kit (GSK), a new open-topped turret kit, seen on the vehicle pictured, provided some armour protection for the machine-gunner's sides and rear. It was referred to as the Gunner's Protection Kit (GPK). (*Brent Sauer*)

(*Opposite page*) An overhead photograph of the forward-facing Gunner's Shield Kit (GSK) and the Gunner's Protection Kit (GPK) on the turret of an M1114 UAH in Iraq. The vehicle's weapon operator is manning an M240 machine gun, which fires a 7.62mm bullet. In theory, the M240 can fire 750 rounds per minute. The realistic rate of fire of the weapon is approximately 100 rounds per minute, to prevent it from overheating. (*DOD*)

(*Right*) Having been unloaded in Kuwait, a number of US Army M1114 UAHs are prepped for their journey to Iraq. Visible are the two rows of vents for the vehicle's built-in air-conditioning unit located on the left-hand side of the vehicle's hatchback enclosure, which are open in this photograph. The M1114 UAH is listed as having the ability to accelerate from 0 to 50mph in 26.1 seconds. (*DOD*)

(*Opposite above*) The US Air Force adopted a slightly modified version of the US Army's M1114 UAH they labelled as the M1116 UAH. An example is shown being decontaminated during a Nuclear, Biological and Chemical (NBC) training exercise. The turret seen in this photograph was unique to the M1116 UAH and consisted of an upper and lower portion. Pictorial evidence indicates that the upper portion of the turret was not always fitted. (*DOD*)

(*Above*) On duty at an air base in Iraq is a US Air Force M1116 UAH. They are employed by US Air Force Security Force units. Unlike the hatchback rear enclosure of the M1114, that of the M1116 is a square-back enclosure as seen in this photograph. The turret on the vehicle is improvised and was named the 'Chavis Turret' after an airman weapon operator on an M1116 was killed by a sniper during the Iraq Insurgency. (*DOD*)

(*Opposite below*) Patrolling an urban area in Iraq is a trio of US Air Force M1116 UAHs, as is evident by the square-back enclosure barely visible on the vehicle in the foreground. The vehicles are fitted with the Objective Gunner's Protection Kit (O-GPK) with the Overhead Cover (OHC) installed. The device projecting out of the front of the vehicle is a Rhino Convoy Protection Device. (*DOD*)

(*Above*) Another US Air Force Humvee variant is the M1145 UAH, which provides both the mobility and protection needed by the US Air Force Enlisted Terminal Attack Controllers (ETACs). Besides supporting battlefield commanders with close-air-support guidance, they also have a level of expertise in both artillery and naval gunfire support. (*DOD*)

(*Opposite above*) An example of the improvised armour arrangements that cropped up on many American military non-armoured and armoured HMMWVs with the beginning of the Iraqi Insurgency in 2003. Visible are locally obtained steel armoured plates mounted on either side of the rear compartment of a HMMWV cargo/troop carrier, as well as locally built steel armoured doors. (*DOD*)

(*Opposite below*) The US Army's short-term solution to the need for better-protected HMMWVs in Iraq was the application of something referred to as the Armor Survivability Kit (ASK), seen here on an M1025 Armament Carrier. The four-door ASK added 1,300lbs to a HMMWV armament carrier, such as the M1025 or M1026. Besides new armoured doors, the ASK included under-body protection. (*Brent Sauer*)

139

With the encasing of the occupants of HMMWVs in Iraq with the Armor Survivability Kit (ASK) came the need to provide them with air-conditioning. To address this issue, the US Army purchased commercial truck air-conditioning units from the Red Dot Corporation. An example of the Red Dot air-conditioning system is shown mounted on the rear hatchback enclosure of an M1025 Armament Carrier. *(Brent Sauer)*

This US Army M1025 or M1026 HMMWV armament carrier in Iraq is fitted with the Armor Survivability Kit (ASK). Notice the thickness of the ballistic glass in the foreground that forms part of the armoured door, an external spotting feature of the ASK. The ASK was designed to provide protection for vehicle occupants from both 7.62mm ammunition and improvised explosive devices. *(DOD)*

Taken during the Iraqi Insurgency is this picture of a US Army HUMMWV two-door cargo/troop carrier fitted with ASK. On either side of the rear compartment of the vehicle are what appear to be locally acquired scrap steel plates held in place by brackets. For additional protection, the soldiers have placed Kevlar blankets on the outside and inside of the rear compartment. (DOD)

Rolling down an Iraqi road is a two-door USMC cargo/troop carrier fitted with the Marine Corps Armor Kit (MAK). The protection provided by the MAK comes from a combination of different types of steel armours and thick ballistic glass all around the cab. Instead of the single thick ballistic glass vision port seen in the doors of US Army ASK-equipped HMMWVs, the MAK-supplied armoured doors each have two ballistic glass vision ports. (DOD)

(*Opposite above*) An overhead photograph of a two-door USMC cargo/troop carrier fitted with the Marine Corps Armor Kit (MAK). Notice the Red Dot air-conditioning unit on the cab roof of the vehicle. The MAK was designed to be modular in design and could provide a minimum level of protection, with 1,800lbs of extra armour protection for cargo/troop carriers. (*DOD*)

(*Above*) Marines with guns drawn dismounting from an M1043A2 Armament Carrier fitted with the Marine Armor Kit (MAK). The tall vertical turret design was unique to the USMC armament carriers fitted with the MAK. Full protection for armament carriers fitted with the MAK came at the price of an extra 3,400lbs. (*DOD*)

(*Opposite below*) A young Marine crouched in front of a USMC M1114 in Iraq. The elaborate turret on the roof of the vehicle is referred to as the Marine Corps Transparent Armored Gun Shield (MCTAGS), which replaced the rather crude turret design that came with the MAK. The two thick ballistic glass vision ports seen on each of the two armoured doors identify it as being fitted with the MAK. (*DOD*)

(*Above*) The replacement for the M1114 UAH was the M1151 series UAH, seen here during a US Army training exercise. It was intended to be built with the basic armour package seen on this vehicle, labelled as the 'A Kit'. Notice it is fitted with the original bullet-resistant (not bullet-proof) doors of the A0 through A2 legacy HMMWV series armament/TOW carriers. (*DOD*)

(*Opposite above*) At a staging area are a number of US Army National Guard M1151 series UAHs. They are fitted with the up-armour 'B3 Kit', as indicated by the single thick horizontal oriented ballistic glass vision port in each armoured door. In comparison, the ballistic glass vision ports that came with the US Army ASK or the UMSC MAK were both smaller and vertically-oriented. (*DOD*)

(*Opposite below*) This USMC M1151A1 UAH is fitted with the up-armour B3 Kit. An identifying feature of the entire M1151 series UAHs is the wire-mesh covering for the horizontally-oriented air-conditioning intake located at the rear of the cargo bay just above the rear tyre. There is another one in the same location on the other side of the vehicle. (*DOD*)

(*Above*) In this picture taken during a training exercise is a USMC M1151A1 UAH in the foreground. It is fitted with the up-armour B3 Kit that allowed for the ballistic glass windows to be opened by being slid out sideways on an upper and lower track. The vehicle is fitted with the Marine Corps Transparent Armored Gun Shield (MCTAGS). (*DOD*)

(*Opposite above*) Moving through a field during a training exercise is an M1167A1 UAH in the foreground, fitted with the up-armour B3 Kit. The M1167A1 UAH is a sub-variant of the M1151 UAH series. It is armed with the TOW Improved Target Acquisition System (ITAS). Prior to firing the missile, the operator lowers the rear armour panel of his open-topped turret to vent the back-blast from the weapon. (*DOD*)

(*Opposite below*) Despite the outstanding mobility capabilities of the entire HMMWV series it is possible to render them immobile, as is evident with this picture of a US Army M1151A1 UAH in Afghanistan, fitted with an up-armour B3 kit. Located at the rear of the vehicle is a Counter Remote Controlled Improvised Explosive Device (RCIED). On the roof of the vehicle is the open-topped Objective Gunners Protective Kit (O-GPK). (*DOD*)

(*Opposite above*) Driving off a US Navy landing craft is a USMC M1151A1 UAH fitted with the Marine Corps Transparent Armored Gun Shield (MCTAGS). The vehicle is fitted with the up-armour B3 kit. To facilitate the driving of its HMMWV fleet on and off the steep ramps of US Navy landing craft, the USMC had all of them constructed without the rear bumpers which appear on the other services, HMMWV inventories. (*DOD*)

(*Above*) This photograph taken at a US Army reclamation yard in Iraq shows the door of a badly-damaged M1151A1 UAH being torn-off by a steel cable during a training exercise. What is interesting in this picture is the improvised transparent armour cover fitted over the standard Gunner's Protection Kit (GPK). The improvised turret roof was made from the ballistic windshields of destroyed M1114 series UAHs. (*DOD*)

(*Opposite below*) Having just arrived at its designation by ship, this M1151A1 UAH has not yet been issued to its unit. The vehicle is fitted with the up-armour B3 Kit and features a factory-designed and built FRAG 7 turret arrangement. This consists of the open-topped Objective Gunner's Protection Kit (O-GPK) fitted with a new overhead armour component labelled as the Overhead Cover (OHC). (*DOD*)

Other than developing ever-more elaborately constructed turrets for the weapon operators on armoured HMMWVs such as the M1114 and M1151 UAHs, the US Army adopted for some of its UAH inventory a device pictured here known as the Common Remotely Operated Weapons Station (CROWS). It can be fitted with a variety of weapons. (*DOD*)

As seen in this picture, the Common Remotely Operated Weapons Station (CROWS) mounted on the M1114 UAH is operated by a gunner located in a rear passenger seat of the vehicle. The weapon mount is stabilized and provides a fire-on-the-move capability. The mount includes a thermal camera as well as a laser rangefinder. (*DOD*)

Because the insurgents in Iraq never stopped developing ever-more powerful roadside IEDs, a call came to up-armour the doors of the M1114 UAHs. This prompted the development of an interim FRAG 5, seen here on the door of a M1114 UAH pictured somewhere in Iraq. The turret on this vehicle is the standard open-topped Gunner Protection Kit (GPK) fitted with a non-standard transparent gun shield. *(DOD)*

This picture taken in Iraq is of an M1114 UAH in UMSC service. It can be readily identified as an M1114 UAH rather than the M1151 series UAH by the air-conditioning vents on the right side of the vehicle's rear hatchback enclosure. The vehicle is fitted with the standard FRAG 5, identified by the thick armoured doors, which allowed room for the ballistic glass windows to be rolled down. *(DOD)*

An Iraqi Army Special Operation Forces (SOF) modified M1114 UAH with FRAG 5 that may have been passed down to them by an American SOF unit. The standard rear hatchback enclosure has been removed, and in its place is an open-topped armour-protected seating area with steps at the rear of the vehicle. The vertical door latches on the FRAG 5 are unique and are a spotting feature. *(DOD)*

A USMC training exercise in Iraq during the insurgency; notice the lack of a magazine in the Marine's M4 rifle seen in the foreground of the picture. In the background is an M1114 UAH fitted with FRAG 5. On the roof of the vehicle is the Objective Gunner's Protection Kit (O-GPK), with an improved sun shield that also made it harder for enemy snipers to identify the weapon operator. *(DOD)*

Two USMC HMMWVs being readied for loading upon a US Navy transport ship. One is a four-door M1165A1 and the other a two-door M1152A1. Both are fitted with the maximum up-armour 'B-3 Kits'. The M1165A1 is classified as a command and control vehicle by the American military. The M1152A1 is suitable for being employed as a troop carrier, cargo carrier or shelter carrier. (*DOD*)

The widespread use of IEDs by the enemy in both Iraq and Afghanistan pushed American Special Operation Forces (SOFs) to take into service an armoured HMMWV based on the M1165A1. It is designated the Ground Mobility Vehicle (GMV). The example pictured belongs to the US Navy SEALs and is labelled as the GMV-N (Navy). (*DOD*)

The American military's replacement for its HMMWV legacy fleet is referred to as the Joint Light Tactical Vehicle (JLTV). Pictured are three different versions of the same vehicle that were submitted by Lockheed Martin for US Army consideration as the JLTV. The JLTV contract calls for as many as 55,000 units of the vehicle to be built in two different models. *(DOD)*

Undergoing US Army testing is the Oshkosh Corporation vehicle that was chosen by the US Army in late August 2015 as the future Joint Light Tactical Vehicle (JLTV). In the configuration shown it is labelled as a Combat Tactical Vehicle (CTV). Based on the same chassis would be another variant referred to as the Combat Support Vehicle (CSV). *(DOD)*

Chapter Five

Post-Cold War Wheeled AFVs

The official end of the Cold War in December 1991 meant the threat of Communism had ceased. In its place appeared a number of other threats to world order, most of those centered in Third World nations. These ranged from religious issues to conflicts over the allocation of natural resources.

As Third World countries typically lacked the infrastructure of first-class roads and heavy bridges which could support the weight of the full-tracked AFVs, the American military was forced to rely on its existing lighter wheeled AFVs for many combat-related duties, and fund the development and fielding of new wheeled AFVs.

A New Armored Car

In 1999, the Textron Marine & Land Systems Corporation, which had acquired Cadillac Gage in 1995, won a contract from the US Army to build ninety-four units of a 4 × 4 vehicle that was standardized as the M1117 Armored Security Vehicle (ASV).

The M1117 ASV was intended as a military police vehicle to replace the US Army's HMMWV armament carriers in security and convoy protection duties. It is armed with a large-calibre machine gun and an automatic grenade launcher.

Due to other funding priorities, the US Army was ready to cancel the M1117 ASV program in 2003. However, with the outbreak of the Iraqi Insurgency and the HMMWV armament carriers (with the basic armoured package) proving unequal to the roles assigned them, the American Congress saved the M1117 ASV program in order to rush more of them to Iraq. Unlike the flat-bottomed HMMWVs, the M1117 ASV had a V-shaped hull to deflect the blast from under-vehicle explosive devices.

By 2007, the US Army had approximately 1,700 units of the M1117 ASV in service. In 2008, the US Army awarded another contract to the Textron Marine & Land Systems Corporation for an additional 329 units, bringing the service inventory to over 2,000 units. In 2008, the US Army began a 'reset' process that returned all of its M1117 ASVs which had served in Iraq and Afghanistan back to like-new condition.

M1117 Variants

In 2009, the Textron Marine & Land Systems Corporation received its first contract from the US Army for the construction of a variant of the M1117 ASV labelled as the

M1200 Armored Knight. It was the replacement for the M707 Knight HMMWV and the full-tracked M981 fire support team vehicle. By 2012, the US Army had acquired 414 of the M1200 Armored Knight out of a planned requirement for 465 units.

A description of the role performed by the US Army M1200 Armored Knight appears in a US Army public affairs document: '... provides precision strike capability by locating and designating targets for both ground and air delivered laser-guided ordnance and conventional munitions.'

Beginning in 2011, the American Government began delivery of approximately 400 units of a modified series of M1117 ASVs in three different versions to the Afghanistan Army. They are referred to as either the Mobile Strike Force Vehicle (MSFV) or the Medium Armored Security Vehicle (MASV).

Indirect Fire Wheeled AFV

In 2003, the American military ordered the first of approximately 400 units of a BAE designed and built vehicle labelled as the High Mobility Artillery Rocket System (HIMARS) M142. The last series production units were delivered in 2013. The launcher unit and rockets/missiles are provided by Lockheed Martin Missile and Fire-Control. The HIMARS is based on a modified 5-ton 6 × 6 truck.

A US Army public affairs document describes the HIMARS: 'The M142 provides responsive, highly accurate, and extremely lethal surface-to-air rocket and missile fire from 15 to 300 kilometres [9 to 186 miles] ... and is operated by a three-man crew protected from launch exhaust/debris and ballistic threats by an armoured man-rated cab.' The vehicle saw combat in both Iraq and Afghanistan with the US Army and USMC.

A First for the US Army

In 1999, the US Army's top general expressed a strong interest in fielding a wheeled AFV series that would form the core of a new type of combat organization originally named the 'Interim Force'. He envisioned that it would fill the void in capability between the service's heavy tank-equipped forces and the light forces which lacked almost any AFVs, and would be deployable anywhere around the world within ninety-six hours by existing US Air Force multi-engine transport planes.

The US Army decided to buy an off-the-shelf design to meet the requirement for an interim wheeled AFV rather than the time-consuming process of developing a suitable vehicle from the ground-up. After testing a number of candidates, the US Army determined in November 2000 that a modified version of an 8 × 8 vehicle designed by the Swiss firm of Motorwagenfabrik AG would meet its needs.

The modified Swiss-designed vehicle chosen by the US Army was labelled by the firm as the 'Piranha III'. It was a larger and improved version of the Piranha I, upon which the USMC LAV family was based. The Piranha III would be built by a partnership of General Motors of Canada and General Dynamics Land Systems (GDLS). In February 2002, the US Army announced that the Piranha III family would be named the 'Stryker' in honor of two Medal of Honor recipients, both with the last name Stryker.

The Stryker Arrives on the Scene

The most numerous model of the Stryker family is the M1126 Infantry Carrier Vehicle (ICV). It can be armed with either a large-calibre machine gun or an automatic grenade launcher. In June 2015, due to long-time concerns by the US Army about the limited lethality of the vehicle's large-calibre machine gun, the American Congress authorized $371 million for the development and acquisition of a 30mm automatic-cannon-armed version of the Stryker.

Other versions of the Stryker family include the M1134 Anti-tank Guided Missile Vehicle (ATGM) equipped with a twin launcher for the TOW 2B, the M1128 Mobile Gun System (MGS) armed with a 105mm main gun, the M1127 Reconnaissance Vehicle (RV) and the M1129A1 Mortar Carrier (MC), which is armed with a 120mm mortar. The vehicle carries onboard a spare 81mm mortar.

Other models in the Stryker family include the M1130 Command Vehicle (CV), the M1131A1 Fire Support Vehicle (FSV), the M1132 Engineer Squad Vehicle (ESV), the M1135 NBC Reconnaissance Vehicle (NBCRV) and the M1133 Medical Evacuation Vehicle (MEV). All except the M1129 MC and M1133 MEV are armed with a large-calibre machine gun for self-defense.

The US Army's rush to field the Stryker family was not without problems with some models, as can be seen in this extract from the 2004 Annual Report by the US Army's Director, Operational Test and Evaluation:

> During the IOT [Initial Operational Test], the ESV [M1132 Engineer Squad Vehicle] could not maintain pace with the other Strykers when equipped with the mine plow or mine roller. The mine roller, lane marketing system, and mine roller performed poorly, and the overall system is prone to failure ... The MGS [M1128 Mobile Gun System] demonstrated poor reliability, excessive weapon system dead space, and other issues associated with gun sights, main gun fire control, and soldier-machine interface.

Despite repeated attempts, the US Army and GDLS could not resolve the design flaws of the M1128 MGS and the service capped production of the vehicle in 2010, with 142 units in service. In its place, the US Army has begun considering the adoption of a full-tracked light tank armed with a 105mm main gun.

In practice, it turned out that the entire premise upon which the acquisition of the Stryker family was based was faulty. This is seen in a 2002 Rand Report titled the *Stryker Brigade Combat Team: Rethinking Strategic Responsiveness and Assessing*

Deployment Options. In that report appears this passage on what the realistic time frame would be for a Stryker unit with all its supporting vehicles to deploy overseas:

> ... the analysis in this report suggests that a force with over 1,000 vehicles cannot be deployed by air from CONUS [Continental United States] to the far reaches of the globe in four days. With some mobility enhancements, it will be possible to achieve deployment timelines on the order of one to two weeks, which is quite rapid for a motorized force.

Protection

The first combat employment of the Stryker family took place during the Iraqi Insurgency, starting in October 2003. Having entered service the year before, the vehicle was designed with a base armour package only proof against large-calibre machine-gun fire on the front of the vehicle and small-calibre machine fire on the remainder of the vehicle. This was indicative of the 'lightness dogma' that prevailed at the senior levels of the US Army that requested in the Stryker family, without factoring in real-world threats to the vehicle.

Concerns about the Stryker family lacking enough protection against the threats it would encounter in Iraq led the US Army to explore up-armouring the vehicle. By the time the first Stryker Brigade Combat Team (SBCT) arrived in Iraq, it had been fitted with two external add-on armour kits. The first consisted of ceramic armour tiles, backed up by thin steel armour plates that would protect it against large-calibre machine-gun fire and artillery airbursts.

The second external add-on armour kit for the Stryker family deployed to Iraq was referred to as 'slat armour'. It was intended to stop rocket propelled grenades (RPGs) from striking the vehicle's hull and was fitted to all Stryker-equipped units in Iraq by December 2003. The background for slat armour can be found in this extract from a book published by the US Army Center for Military History in 2007 and titled *From Transformation to Combat: the First Stryker Brigade at War*:

> American tankers in Vietnam had used chain-link fencing or chicken wire to achieve the same effect against North Vietnamese and Viet Cong rocket grenades [RPG-2 and RPG-7]. Applying those same precedents, the Army tested an updated version of this idea at its Aberdeen Proving Ground in Maryland during July 2003. The solution slat armour, involved the addition of an encircling grid of hardened steel bars to a Stryker's hull to make anti-tank rockets detonate before hitting anything vital. The expedient protected the vehicles much better but added some 2.5 tons of dead weight to each and expanded its girth by close to 3 feet. Although this inevitably affected the Stryker's transportability by aircraft and its manoeuvrability in urban areas, there were no immediate alternatives.

The GDLS slat armour kits fitted to the Strykers in Iraq were originally envisioned as being able to stop the majority of RPG strikes. However, this proved not to be the case, as seen in an internal US Army document released in 2004 that was made public the following year by a nonprofit watchdog group named the Project on Government Oversight. The document title is *Initial Impressions Report, Operations in Mosul, Iraq, Stryker Brigade Combat Team 1, 3rd Brigade, 2nd Infantry*. In it appears this extract regarding the effectiveness of slat armour, or lack of:

> Soldiers were briefed that slat armour would protect them against eight out of eleven strikes against Rocket Propelled Grenade (RPG) attacks. In the field, soldiers say the slat armour is effective against half of the RPG attacks. There are three types of RPG attacks that have been encountered, Anti-Personnel (AP), High Explosive Anti-Tank (HEAT), and Anti-Tank (AT). The AP RPG attacks were not reduced by slat armour because the rocket explodes with shrapnel and is dangerous to the Stryker Vehicle Commander (VC) and air guards … HEAT RPG attacks can be successfully defeated if the rocket hits between the slats because the slat armour affects the shaped charge and prevents it from working properly. AT RPG attacks are not defeated, in most cases, because the penetrator is not affected by the slat armour.

The report also mentions that with the slat armour fitted on Strykers, neither the fuel spouts on the vehicle, or the existing tow bars proved long enough. During accidents or roll-over incidents, the slat armour often crumbled and bent, blocking the crew's escape hatches.

Reactive Armor

The original slat armour kit named 'SLAT I' by General Dynamics Land Systems was only a stop-gap measure, as the initial plans had called for the Stryker family to be fitted with a reactive armour tile kit named 'SRAT II' before deployment to Iraq. SRAT II was developed by General Dynamics Ordnance, and Tactical Systems and Rafael Advanced Defense Systems Ltd, an Israeli firm.

Reactive armour tiles not only provide protection from RPGs, but have the added benefit of offering a certain amount of protection from EFPs, which a slat armour kit would not stop. However, there is no pictorial evidence of SRAT II being fitted to the Stryker series employed in Iraq or Afghanistan. This may have to do with the perceived threat that activated reactive armour tiles could pose to exposed friendly combatants.

The Threat From Below

A serious threat to the Stryker family that served in Iraq and Afghanistan were mines and IEDs. Despite such devices having been the biggest threat to US Army wheeled

AFVs during the Vietnam War, the US Army ordered the Stryker family with flat-bottom hulls, which made them extremely vulnerable.

In an article that appeared in the 20 May 2011 issue of *Stars and Stripes* is this quote from US Army Private Dustyn Applepate, who was riding in a Stryker in Afghanistan when it ran over an extremely large IED in August 2010: 'That's the bad thing about the Stryker. It has a flat bottom, so when the blast happens, it just blows up instead of up and out like an MRAP [Mine Resistant Ambush Protected Vehicle]. There is no safe place on the Stryker.'

In a publication by Combat Studies Institute Press titled *Strykers in Afghanistan 1st Battalion 17th Infantry Regiment in Kandahar Province 2009* appears this more detailed description of what happens when a Stryker encounters a large IED:

> [Captain Adam] Swift was leading a four-vehicle Stryker patrol west of FOB [Forward Operating Base] Frontenac when an IED detonated directly beneath his Stryker, penetrating the hull and ripping off all eight tyres. Swift, who had been standing in the commander's hatch, awoke upside down on the floor. The blast cracked his pelvis and shredded the legs of both Sergeant Tanner Kuth and Specialist Derek Ford, who had been sitting across from each other. The driver, Private First Class Joshua Seaver was knocked unconscious. Men yelled and screamed inside the Stryker as alarms went off. Dust and smoke filled the vehicle. 'There was blood and stuff everywhere,' recalled Smith.

To address the design issue of the Stryker family having a flat-bottom hull, both the US Army and GDLS decided to convert a portion of its Stryker M1126 ICV inventory with a newly-designed Double-V Hull (DVH). Testing confirmed that the DVH provided the M1126 ICVs with an enhanced degree of protection for their crews and passengers from mines and IEDs.

The first of the heavier Stryker DVHs arrived in Afghanistan in 2011 and received generally positive reviews. Besides the new lower hull design, the DVH package includes increased armour protection and, due to the added weight, upgraded suspension and braking systems. Other upgrades include blast-attenuating seats and a height management system (HMS) to increase ground clearance, that improves both vehicle survivability and mobility.

Stryker Designation Changes

If funding permits, the US Army hopes eventually to have the bulk of its inventory of Stryker family upgraded with the DVH package. There were also Strykers that came off the assembly line with the DVH package already fitted. In 2015, the US Army Stryker inventory consisted of approximately 4,000 units.

Reflecting the upgrades that came with the Stryker DVH package, the US Army made minor designation changes to some of its Stryker family. All of those upgraded with the DVH package had an extra 'V' added to their designations. For example, the original M1126 ICV with the flat-bottom hull, when fitted with the DVH package, was re-designated as the M1256 ICVV.

The M1252 Mortar Carrier (MC), the M1255 Command Vehicle (CV), the M1251 Fire Support Vehicle (FSV), the M1257 Engineer Support Vehicle (ESV) and the M1251 Medical Evacuation Vehicle (MEV) all had the letter 'V' added to the end of their existing designations.

The M1134 Anti-tank Guided Missile Vehicle (ATGM) fitted with the DVH package was relabelled as the XM1253 ATVV. A new variant of the M1126 ICVV fitted with the DVH package is referred to as the M1256 ICVV-S, with the last letter standing for 'scout'.

Due to a number of design issues, the US Army decided that the M1128 Mobile Gun System (MGS), the M1135 NBC Reconnaissance Vehicle (NBCRV) and the M1127 Reconnaissance Vehicle (RV) would not be upgraded with the DVH package and therefore retained their existing designations. The M1127 RV performed poorly in combat and was replaced by the M1256 Infantry Carrier Vehicle (DVH) Scout (ICVV-S).

A Stop-Gap Wheeled AFV

Because the American public had become increasingly casualty-averse during the early stages of the Iraqi and Afghan insurgencies, the generals in both theatres of conflict sought wheeled AFVs optimized for protection from mines and IEDs, which is typically provided by V-shaped hulls. These vehicles with the V-shaped hulls were being referred to under the general heading of Mine Resistant Ambush Protected vehicles (MRAPs).

The case for MRAPs can be seen in these extracts from an Urgent Universal Need Statement to the Department of Defense (DOD) by USMC Brigadier General D.J. Hejlik in January 2005:

> There is an immediate need for an MRAP vehicle capability to increase surviv-ability and mobility of Marines operating in a hazardous fire area against known threats … The MRAP will mitigate three primary kill mechanisms of mines and IEDs – fragmentation, blast overpressure, and acceleration. It will also counter the secondary kill mechanisms of vehicle crashes following mine strikes and fire aboard vehicles.

As the DOD acquisition system has always been more oriented toward future opera-tional capabilities, it was not really convinced that the stop-gap and potential costly MRAPs were the answer to the request of General Hejlik and others. This created a four-year gap between the time they were first requested by the field commanders in 2003 and their initial arrival in the theatres of combat in late 2007.

The excuse by the DOD senior leadership that they could not have anticipated the eventual need for MRAPs was rebuffed in one of its own inspector general's reports. A passage from that report is quoted here:

DOD was aware of the threat posed by mines and improvised explosive devices (IEDs) in low-intensity conflicts and the availability of mine-resistant vehicles years before insurgent actions began in Iraq in 2003. Yet DOD did not develop requirements for, fund, or acquire MRAP type vehicles for low-intensity conflicts that involved mines and IEDs. As a result, the Department entered into operations in Iraq without having taken available steps to acquire technology to mitigate the known mine and IED risk to soldiers and Marines.

MRAP Procurement

As the DOD was concerned that MRAP procurement would come at the expense of other high-priority programs, the American Congress and the Secretary of Defense assured the DOD that the MRAPs would be funded separately – so that DOD would make MRAPs the number one priority. Once that occurred, the DOD placed an order for 7,774 MRAPs, subsequently increased to 15,374 units.

From a Congressional Research Service report dated 21 August 2007, that was prepared for members of Congress, appears this extract reflecting some of the concerns about the MRAP program:

Although MRAP vehicles appear to offer significantly more protection than the current fleet of up-armoured HMMWVs, some observers caution that advances in IED design and the use of more sophisticated anti-tank missiles and rocket-propelled grenades (RPGs) could render MRAPs just as vulnerable as up-armoured HMMWVs ... DOD pressure for industry to meet high production goals and competition between vendors could result in MRAP quality control issues.

By the time the MRAP program ended in 2012, approximately 28,000 units had been procured in less than three years. User input from the theatres of combat would result in a constant series of modifications and upgrades to the MRAP fleet to meet the evolving threats posed by the insurgents in Iraq and Afghanistan.

MRAP Types

The DOD divided the MRAPs into three categories, labelled one to three. According to the American military, Category I MRAPs carry between four and six passengers and provide increased mobility and reliability in rough terrain. Category II MRAPs have multi-mission capability because they are larger and therefore can perform such roles as convoy lead, troop transport and ambulance, and can carry as many as ten passengers. The Category III vehicles were only intended to perform route clearance duties.

As no one company could possibly build so many MRAPs within the time demands of the US Army or USMC, a great scramble began, with a number of firms vying for a piece of the massive contract, which eventually came to $50 billion. Numerous candidate vehicles were tested, with some being rejected, including the M1117 ASV, because its ballistic-protection levels failed to meet the requirements set by the USMC. Others were rejected because of various design flaws.

Navistar International Corporation

The biggest winner in the Category I MRAP competition was a 4 × 4 vehicle built by the Navistar International Corporation. It was designated as the M1224 by the US Army, and referred to by the builder as the 'MaxxPro'. The services ordered 1,200 units of the vehicle in 2007.

With the addition of add-on armour kits, the M1224 was designated as the M1224A1 by the US Army and as the 'MaxxPro MEAP Protected' by the builder. The acronym 'MEAP' stood for MRAP Expedient Armor Program. The add-on armour was primarily aimed at defeating improvised explosively-formed penetrators (EFPs) employed by the enemy in Afghanistan and Iraq.

The next up-armoured version of the MaxxPro series was designated as the M1234 by the US Army, and referred to by the builder as the 'MaxxPro Plus'. To deal with the weight imposed by all the extra armour, the company added dual rear wheels to the vehicle, and a more powerful engine, making it a 6 × 4.

There were also 250 units ordered of a recovery version of the MaxxPro series, designated by the US Army as the M1249 or MRAP Recovery Vehicle (MRV).

Not wanting to miss a sales opportunity, Navistar International submitted a larger and heavier version of their MaxxPro in the Category II of MRAPs. The vehicle was labelled as the 'MaxxPro XL' by the builder. It was never assigned an M number because it was not taken into US Army service. The USMC acquired sixteen units of the vehicle, which served with bomb disposal detachments. They labelled it as the Joint Explosive Ordnance Disposal Rapid Response Vehicle (JERRV).

A New Variant of the MaxxPro

In September 2008, the USMC ordered from Navistar International 822 units of a lighter, smaller and more mobile version of the original MaxxPro, which the builder named the 'MaxxPro Dash' and the US Army designated as the M1235. In December 2008, the USMC placed a second order for 400 additional units.

In 2010, the USMC ordered 1,275 units of an improved version of the MaxxPro Dash with an upgraded suspension system, which the US Army designated as the M1235A1. The builder labelled it as the 'MaxxPro Dash DXM'.

In 2011, the USMC ordered 250 units of an ambulance version of the MaxxPro Dash DXM, which the US Army designated as the M1266A1. That same year the USMC ordered another 471 units of the M1235A1 MaxxPro Dash DXM.

When fitted with the Objective Gunners Protection Kit (OGPK), the US Army designated the M1235A1 as the M1235A4, and when armed with the Common Remotely Weapon Station (CROWS) its designation changes to M1235A5.

BAE Systems

BAE Systems, Inc was the supplier to the American military of a number of MRAPs. One of them was a 6 × 6 MRAP referred to by the firm as the 'Caiman'. It was based on the chassis of a standard American military cargo truck.

Originally the Caiman family was envisioned as a Category II MRAP by the American military. However, as the MRAPs categories are defined by the number of personnel carried onboard and not wheel arrangement, and the majority of 6 × 6 Caimans were delivered with a four-passenger seating arrangement, most fell within the Category I MRAP definition and are listed as such in official American military documents.

The US Army standardized the Category I Caiman as the M1220. An up-armoured version of the Category I Caiman was referred to as the 'Super Caiman'. In total, 2,868 units of the Caiman were built by the time production ended in 2008. As with all the other MRAPs acquired by the American military, it was upgraded and modified by feedback from the user community in the field.

The final model of the Caiman family had a large vertical passive armour panel affixed to either side of the vehicle's hull, and with a ten-person capacity was listed as a Category II MRAP. In this configuration it was standardized by the US Army as the M1230. The builder referred to it as the 'Caiman Plus', or Caiman Tactical Vehicle System (TVS). There was to be a Caiman Multi-Terrain Vehicle (MTV) version, but this was later cancelled by the US Army before production began.

MRAP Lack of M Numbers

The MRAP program started under the auspices of the USMC, and later became a joint program with the US Army. Because the US Army decided to wait until it could determine what MRAPs it wanted to keep in the force structure, there was not a POR assigned to them at first, therefore they went without M numbers. Only when the US Army decided what MRAPs they wished to retain (in severely diminished numbers) were some of the existing vehicles assigned M numbers. The USMC does not employ a POR and its vehicles therefore lack an M number.

Other BAE MRAPs

In 2007, BAE Systems Inc. was awarded a contract to supply a Category I MRAP vehicle designated as the RG-31. BAE arranged to have GDLS oversee procurement of the vehicle. The American military acquired 2,260 units of the RG-31 Medium Mine Protected Vehicle (MMPV) Type II series. There was also a Special Operation Command (SOCOM) variant referred to as the 'RG-31 SOCOM'.

The RG-31 series of vehicles was followed into production by an improved model designated as the RG-33. It was also considered a 4 × 4 Category I MRAP. An up-armoured model was labelled as the 'RG-33 Plus'. BAE also came up with a larger 6 × 6 Category II model labelled as the 'RG-33L'.

Besides use as an infantry transport vehicle, there was a Heavy Armored Ground Ambulance (HAGA) version of the RG-33 and an Armored Utility Vehicle (AUV) version. Total production of the RG-33 series amounted to approximately 1,700 units.

Force Protection Inc.

A small company named Force Protection Inc (FPI), which was formed out of two other small existing firms in 2002, began marketing a 4 × 4 and a 6 × 6 AFV, both of which were referred to as the 'Cougar'. The vehicles pre-dated the MRAP program, which did not begin until 2007. The design of the FPI Cougar was based on a South Africa-designed 4 × 4 wheeled AFV named the 'Lion'.

The first example of the FPI Cougar 4 × 4 and 6 × 6 AFVs debuted in April 2004. The USMC ordered twenty-eight units of the 4 × 4 Cougar Hardened Engineer Vehicle (HEV) that were delivered in late 2004. The USMC ordered 122 units of the 6 × 6 version of the Cougar configured as a JERRV.

In 2006, an order for 280 additional units of the 6 × 6 Cougar was placed for use by the USMC/US Navy Seabees and the US Army. These were all to be employed in the JERRV role.

With the start of the MRAP program the 4 × 4 Cougar was classified as a Category I vehicle and the 6 × 6 Cougar a Category II vehicle. In 2007, the American military ordered 365 units of the 4 × 4 Category I Cougar, now referred to as the Cougar H MRAP, and 760 units of the 6 × 6 Category II Cougar, now labelled as the Cougar HE MRAP, intended for engineering units.

Unfortunately, FPI generally failed to deliver the MRAPs contracted for on their assigned schedule. The seriousness of this issue was addressed in this passage from a June 2007 report by the DOD Inspector General, as well as the services awarding the firm sole source contracts for the vehicles:

> A decision to execute a rapid acquisition by contracting with a company that
> has not demonstrated acceptable performance and responsibility may not be in

the best interest of the Government. In addition, late delivery of the armoured vehicles to theatre may hinder the warfighters' ability to execute mission requirements and increase risk to soldiers' lives.

No doubt in response to the DOD Inspector General Report, FPI sub-contracted with GDLS to build the vehicles they could not in 2007. Follow-on orders from the American military brought the total number of Cougar vehicles to approximately 4,000 units by the time production ceased in 2012. In 2011, GDLS bought Force Protection Inc.

Like all the other MRAPs, the Cougar family was up-armoured in response to user feedback. In addition, to improve the vehicle's off-road mobility the bulk of the fleet was rebuilt with an independent suspension system (ISS). These rebuilt vehicles are labelled by GDLS as the 'Cougar ISS'.

Category III MRAP

As with the Cougar family, FPI had also developed another modified South African designed vehicle for possible sale to the American military prior to the MRAP program beginning. That vehicle was a 6 × 6 referred to as the Buffalo Mine Protected Clearance Vehicle (MPCV). The US Army ordered ten Buffalo MPVCs in 2002, which were delivered in 2003. The same year, the US Army opted for an additional order of seventy-seven units. The Buffalo MPCV was originally intended to be fielded only by US Army engineering units, with the service organizing three route clearance companies per year starting in the Fiscal Year 2007, for a total of twelve companies.

In 2006, the USMC ordered eighty-two units of the Buffalo MPCV. With the beginning of the MRAP program the Buffalo MPCV was labelled as a Category III MRAP. It would be the only Category III MRAP acquired by the American military. In 2009, an improved version of the Buffalo MPCV appeared and was designated the 'A2' by the US Army and the Mk 2 version by the USMC. This resulted in the original model being labelled as the 'A1' by the US Army and the Mk II by the USMC.

By the time series production of the Buffalo MPCV family came to an end in 2014, approximately 650 units of the vehicle had been built, with the majority being the A2/Mk II model. As with the Cougar family of MRAPs, FPI was unable to deliver the Buffalo MPCV family by the dates specified in their contracts.

MRAP Design Problems

The entire series of MRAP vehicles were designed with a high chassis in order to disperse the blast from under-vehicle explosions. The drawback to this design feature was the fact that the MRAPs tended to be top heavy and were therefore very prone to roll-over accidents. This issue was addressed in this passage from a May 2013 report by the US Army Aeromedical Research Laboratory:

An MRAP is prone to roll over on unstable and uneven terrain and come into contact with low-hanging power lines often encountered in theatre ... Analysis of 420 MRAP accidents occurring from November 2007 through August 2009 showed 178 (42 percent) of these accidents involved some type of rollover, resulting in 215 rollover injuries. Additional injuries resulted from falls within the vehicle or being crushed or lacerated by one of the vehicle's heavy armoured components, including doors, ramps, gunner hatches, or the Rhino detonator on the vehicle's front end. Also, 16 (4 percent) of these accidents involved contact with power lines.

From an internal USMC safety newsletter dated June 2008, which was obtained by *Army Times*, comes this extract warning the drivers of MRAPs: 'This ain't your father's Oldsmobile ... Road shoulders in the Middle East do not meet US standards and may collapse under the weight of the MRAP, especially when the road is above grade and can fall to lower ground.'

In spite of the many design issues that came with the fielding of the MRAPs, many soldiers and Marines who served in combat felt much safer in the MRAPs than the various up-armoured models of the HMMWV when confronting enemy mines and IEDs. According to Kris Osborn, an American defence official, quoted in *Defense News* on 6 October 2008: 'Compared to an up-armoured Humvee against the same type of explosive, nine times out of ten there are no injuries in an MRAP other than bumps, bruises and scrapes. And we're talking about a sizable amount of explosives.'

Not Officially an MRAP

An MRAP-like 4 × 4 vehicle that was never actually classified as such by the American military was developed and built by Oshkosh Defense and labelled as the MRAP-All Terrain Vehicle (M-ATV). It was designated as the M1240 by the US Army.

One of the reasons for the fielding of the M-ATV can be found in this quote by Pentagon Press Secretary Geoff Morrel released by the American Forces Press Service on 30 September 2009: 'These new vehicles are urgently needed, because improvised explosive devices are claiming the lives of more US and coalition forces in Afghanistan than ever before. The hope is that the M-ATVs will have the same impact in Afghanistan as the MRAPs did in Iraq.'

The M-ATV was also needed because the larger and heavier MRAPs proved unable to deal with Afghanistan's harsh terrain. Between 2010 and 2012, the US military acquired approximately 8,000 units of the M-ATV in a number variants. As with all the official MRAPs, combat experience led to its quick up-armouring.

When fitted with the Objective Gunners Protection Kit (O-GPK), the M-ATV becomes the M1240A1. Armed with the CROWS it becomes the M1274. Depending on what type of tactical battlefield communication systems it is fitted with, the M1240 can be either designated as the M1276 or the M1277.

MRAP Future

The number of MRAPs that the American military plans on retaining in the inventory has varied from 8,000 to 12,000 units, depending on the sources cited. At the present time, some are slated for active duty units, others for training purposes, and many more have been placed into storage. If funding allows, the American military hopes to retire the last MRAP from the inventory by 2022, when enough units of the JLTV enter service.

Pre-MRAP Gun Trucks

Before the introduction of the MRAPs into Iraq, the US Army fielded a small number of improvised gun trucks armed with a number of machine guns. They were based on the service's standard 6 × 6 5-ton trucks, and were a modern update of those gun trucks that appeared during the Vietnam War.

Development of a standardized 5-ton gun truck for service in Iraq was a joint venture by the Lawrence Livermore National Laboratory and the Defense Advanced Research Projects Agency. Work began in 2003 and deliveries commenced in 2005. Due to their connection with the Lawrence Livermore National Laboratory, they were nicknamed the 'Livermore Gun Trucks'.

(*Opposite page*) A US Army Military Police M1117 Armored Security Vehicle (ASV) on patrol in Iraq. It has a single-person powered turret armed with both a large-calibre machine gun and an automatic grenade launcher. Visible at the rear of the vehicle is an antenna for the AN/ULQ-35 CREW Duke System. On the rear of the turret is one of the vehicle's two smoke grenade launcher units. (*DOD*)

(*Above*) The M1117 Armored Security Vehicle (ASV) has a crew of three and can carry a single passenger. It has a length of 19.9 feet, a width of 8.4 feet and a height of 8.5 feet. The vehicle weighs 29,500lb and is powered by an engine that generates 276hp, which can propel it at a maximum speed on roads of 63mph. (*Textron Marine & Land Systems*)

(*Opposite above*) Seen prior to going on convoy protection duties in Iraq is the rear of a US Army Military Police M1117 Armored Security Vehicle (ASV). The vehicle's general configuration matches that of the late-production units of the Cadillac Gage M706 Commando armoured car, with two-piece armoured doors on either side of the vehicle's hull and another located in the rear of the hull. (*William Garrick*)

(*Above*) The large tyres on the M1117 Armored Security Vehicle (ASV) pictured have run-flat inserts. Besides its steel armoured hull, the vehicle is also protected by ceramic composite appliqué armour and interior spall liners that provide protection from large-calibre machine-gun fire. In addition, the M1117 can withstand the overhead blast and fragments from a 155mm shell and an under-vehicle mine blast of up to 12lbs. (*Textron Marine & Land Systems*)

(*Opposite below*) There were a number of proposed vehicles based on the chassis of the M1117 Armored Security Vehicle (ASV), including a stretched armoured personnel carrier, a mortar carrying version and a command and control model. As of 2016, the only other variant of the M1117 ASV built for the US Army is the M1200 Armored Knight, two of which are seen here. (*DOD*)

(*Opposite page*) Two crewmen of a US Army M1200 Armored Knight are observing the effects of artillery fire during a training exercise. Located in the open-topped armour turret of the vehicle is the Fire Support Sensor System (FS3). The various electronic devices contained with the FS3 are employed by Field Artillery Combat Observation and Lasing Teams (COLT) to direct artillery fire for US Army ground force units. (*DOD*)

(*Right*) For the Afghan Army, the US Government authorized the delivery of a large number of a modified version of the M1117 Armored Security Vehicle (ASV) called the Mobile Strike Force Vehicle. As seen in this picture, it was fitted with the open-topped Objective Gunners Protective Kit (O-GPK) originally developed for the US Army's M1114 and M1151 series of UAHs. (*DOD*)

(*Below*) Two examples of the US Army's M142 High Mobility Artillery Rocket System (HIMARS). It can carry either six unguided surface-to surface rockets or a single ground-to-ground guided missile in the large pod located behind the vehicle's cab. The vehicle's three-man crew is protected by an armoured cab from the engine exhaust flames and gases when the rockets or missiles are launched. (*DOD*)

(*Opposite above*) A rear view of the US Army's M142 High Mobility Artillery Rocket System (HIMARS) fitted with a launching pod containing unguided ground-to-ground rockets, as indicated by the six engine exhaust ports visible. The launcher pod is mounted on a modified 5-ton Family of Medium Tactical Vehicles (FMTV) 6 × 6 chassis. (*DOD*)

(*Opposite below*) On a US Army firing range, an M142 High Mobility Artillery Rocket System (HIMARS) has raised its launching pod into firing position. When firing the unguided ground-to-ground rockets, their flight trajectory depends on the elevation of the launcher pod. The pod with the rockets or missile is raised and lowered hydraulically. (*DOD*)

(*Above*) A factory shot of the original version of the US Army M1126 Stryker Infantry Carrier Vehicle (ICV). Visible at the front hull of the vehicle is the vertical wire-cutter bar. Alongside the vehicle's hull are the storage racks for the vehicle's crew and passengers' belongings, such as sleeping bags. The M1126 (ICV) is 22 feet 11 inches in length, has a width of 8 feet 11 inches and a height of 8 feet 8 inches. (*GDLS*)

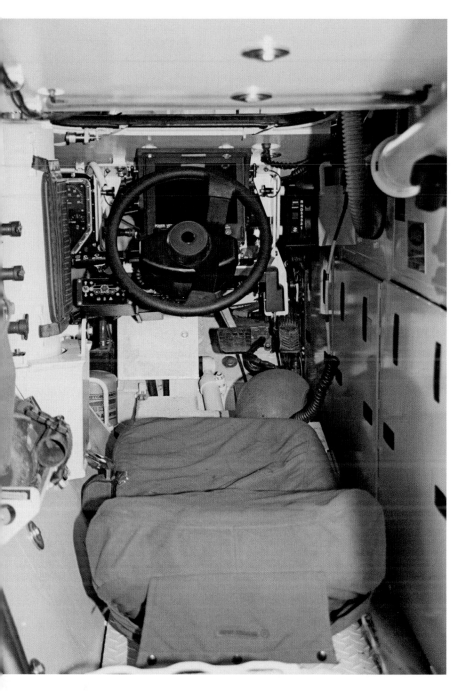

(*Left*) The driver's seat of an M1126 Stryker ICV, with the driver's seat-back in its lowered position. The vehicle is powered by a 350hp engine that can propel it to a maximum speed of 62mph on roads. It is the same engine that powers the American military's Medium Tactical Vehicle Family (MTVF) of 5-ton trucks. (*DOD*)

(*Opposite above*) An important design parameter of the original Stryker series was the ability to be deployed by air anywhere in the world within a certain time frame. In this image is an M1126 Stryker ICV in the very tight confines of a US Air Force C-130 Hercules series four-engine prop-driven transport plane. (*DOD*)

(*Opposite below*) An M1126 Stryker ICV being directed into the spacious cargo hold of a US Air Force C-17 Globemaster jet-engine transport plane. The original version of the M1126 ICV weighed 38,000lbs combat loaded, and would be lightened as much as possible prior to being loaded onto any of the Air Force's transport aircraft. (*DOD*)

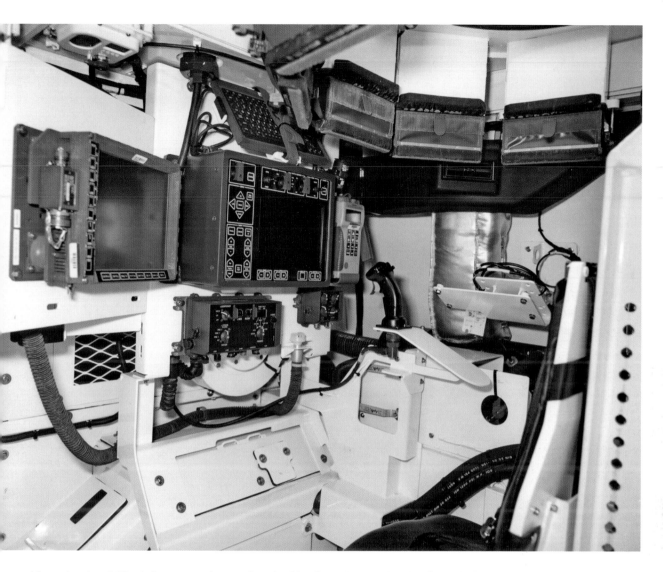

(*Opposite above*) The infantry squad seen disembarking from the rear hatch of an M1126 Stryker ICV consisted of nine men. They sit on two bench seats in the rear hull of the vehicle, four on one side and five on the other. There are no vision-ports or gun-ports in the M1126 ICV hull from which the onboard infantrymen can fire their personal weapons. (*DOD*)

(*Above*) Besides the driver of the M1126 Stryker ICV, there is a vehicle commander who operates the roof-mounted remote-control weapon, labelled as the Remote Weapons Station (RWS). The vehicle commander aims and fires the RWS with the aid of the larger of the two video monitors seen in this picture. (*DOD*)

(*Opposite below*) The Remote Weapon Station (RWS) seen in this factory photo of an M1126 Stryker ICV can be armed with either the large-calibre machine gun pictured or an automatic grenade launcher. Combat experience has showed that the various optical devices and sensors that make up the RWS are extremely vulnerable to many battlefield threats. (*GDLS*)

(*Opposite above*) Once it was realized that the Stryker series would be deployed to take part in countering the Iraqi Insurgency, there began a mad rush to increase the vehicle's protection level. This would result in a slat armour kit being developed for the vehicle, as seen on this M1126 Stryker ICV. Combat experience in Iraq soon showed that the slat armour kit was poorly designed and did not provide as much protection as advertised. (*DOD*)

(*Above*) The slat armour kits on these two M1126 Stryker Infantry Carrier Vehicles (ICVs) pictured in Iraq were intended as an interim measure only. They were to remain in use until such time as a suitable add-on ceramic armour tile kit could be developed for the vehicle. The original German-designed and built ceramic armour tiles proved defective and were rejected by the US Army. (*DOD*)

(*Opposite below*) The M1126 Stryker ICVs in the foreground and background are both fitted with slat armour kits. Visible on the camouflaged sand-painted Stryker in the foreground are the large exterior studs that identify it as being fitted with the German-designed and built ceramic armour tile kit. (*DOD*)

(*Above*) In this overhead picture of an M1126 Stryker ICV on patrol in Iraq can be seen the various roof features of the vehicle. There is the vehicle commander's cupola on the right-hand side of the forward portion of the hull. To the left of that is the overhead hatch for the squad leader. At the rear of the roof are two overhead hatches for what are referred to as the 'air guards'. (*DOD*)

(*Opposite above*) The ultimate version of the M1126 Stryker ICV employed in Iraq. Notice the armoured skirting along the lower hull to provide a bit more protection for the vehicle's large tyres. There is a large camouflaged structure on the rear roof of the vehicle to hide the exposed passengers from sniper fire. (*DOD*)

(*Opposite below*) Taken during a US Army training exercise, this photograph shows two examples of the Stryker M1134 Anti-tank Guided Missile Vehicle (ATGM). The head of the elevated armoured launcher unit is armed with two TOW 2B missiles on one side and the optics for aiming and firing the missiles on the other side. Notice the large rear ramp common to all the Stryker series, with a built-in door. (*DOD*)

In this company photograph is a Stryker M11134 Anti-tank Guided Missile Vehicle (ATGM) with its TOW 2B launcher unit in the retracted position. The vehicle has a four-man crew: driver, vehicle commander, weapon operator and loader. Once the two missiles in the armoured launcher are fired, the loader in the rear hull compartment must be exposed to reload them, which takes about two minutes. (*GDLS*)

A TOW B2 missile has just left the armoured launcher pod of a Stryker M11134 Anti-tank Guided Missile Vehicle (ATGM) on a test range. The vehicle is equipped with two types of TOW 2B missiles. One is optimized as an anti-tank weapon and the other for bunker busting. The missiles themselves have a maximum range of approximately 4,000 yards. (*DOD*)

Mounted on the forward roof of the Stryker M1131 Fire Support Vehicle (FSV) is the Fire Support Sensor System (FS3) employed to direct artillery fire. The vehicle has a four-man crew and can be identified by the lack of a Remote Weapon Station (RWS). In its place is a manually-operated large-calibre machine gun. (*DOD*)

Two examples of the Stryker M1129 Mortar Carrier (MC-B) during a training exercise. The rear compartment of the vehicle was widened, as is evident in this picture, to make room for the very large 120mm mortar. When not in use, a two-piece overhead armoured hatch, seen in this picture, covers the lowered mortar. (*DOD*)

(*Opposite above*) In this wide-angle view is the rear interior compartment of the Stryker M1129 Mortar Carrier (MC-B). The mortar is fitted to a 360 degree turntable mount, allowing it to be quickly set to fire in a different direction when called upon. The vehicle has authorized storage room for sixty rounds of ammunition, including high-explosive (HE) and white phosphorus smoke. (*DOD*)

(*Opposite below*) A Stryker M1129 Mortar Carrier (MC-B) in action during a training exercise. The 120mm mortar has a maximum range of 7,918 yards. To increase its battlefield effectiveness, the vehicle is equipped with an onboard fire-control computer with an inertial navigation and pointing system. This allows the mortar crews to fire in under a minute, improving lethality and crew survivability. (*DOD*)

(*Above*) Taking part in a training exercise is this Stryker M1130 Command Vehicle (CV). The number of radio antennas fitted to the vehicle can vary depending on the mission. It has a crew of two – the driver and the vehicle commander – and can carry up to four passengers. Like the M1131 Fire Support Vehicle (FSV), it is not fitted with the Remote Weapon Station (RWS). Instead, it is fitted with a manually-operated large-calibre machine gun. (*DOD*)

(*Opposite above*) Taking part in a training exercise is a Stryker M1132 Engineer Squad Vehicle (ESV) fitted with an Angled Mine Plow (AMP). The role of the vehicle is to breach minefields to allow the safe passage of other vehicles. To indicate the cleared path for the follow-on vehicles, the M1132 ESV is fitted with a lane marking system at the rear of the vehicle. Besides the driver and vehicle commander, the vehicle carries a nine-man squad of engineers. (*DOD*)

(*Opposite below*) An M1132 Engineer Squad Vehicle (ESV) fitted with a mine roller. US Army tactics call for the M1132 ESV fitted with a mine plow to be the first to breach a minefield under cover of smoke. This is done after firing a Mine-Clearing Line Charge (MCLC) carried in a trailer normally towed behind the vehicle. It will then be followed by an M1132 ESV fitted with the mine roller. (*DOD*)

(*Above*) A Stryker M1135 Nuclear, Biological and Chemical (NBC) Reconnaissance Vehicle (NBCRV). Its job is to identify NBC contaminated areas and alert all other units to its presence by various means. The mast-like device visible just behind the Remote Weapon Station (RWS) is referred to as the Joint Service Lightweight Standoff Chemical Agent Detector (JSLSCAD). (*DOD*)

(*Opposite above*) Two members of the four-man crew of a Stryker M1135 Nuclear Biological Chemical Reconnaissance Vehicle (NBCRV) are seen in full protective gear practicing how to decontaminate their vehicle. At the rear of the vehicle is a device referred to as the Double Wheel Sampling System, which allows for the collection of contaminated ground samples while the vehicle is moving. (*DOD*)

(*Opposite below*) As is evident by the markings on the vehicle, it is a Stryker M1133 Medical Evacuation Vehicle (MEV). To provide the maximum room in the rear of the vehicle for the care of the wounded, the walls on either side have been widened. In addition, the roof of the rear compartment on the M1133 MEV has also been raised, something not seen on any other Stryker models. (*DOD*)

(*Above*) In this factory shot is the most troublesome version of the Stryker series, designated as the M1128 Mobile Gun System (MGS). It is armed with a 105mm main gun in a remote-control turret supplied with ammunition by an 18-round automatic loader in the rear of the turret. Another twelve main gun rounds are stored in the vehicle's hull. (*GDLS*)

At the moment of firing is the 105mm main gun on the three-man M1128 Mobile Gun System (MGS). The main gun is the same as was fitted to the M60 series of main battle tanks and the first-generation M1 Abrams tank. Such is the recoil of this powerful weapon that it would roll-over the M1128 MGS if fired on a side slope. To fill the automatic loader when empty would require a member of the crew to expose himself on the roof of the vehicle. *(GDLS)*

The original model of the Category 1 MaxxPro MRAP designed and built by Navistar International Corporation, which can be identified by the vertical engine grill slats. It was designated as the M1224 by the US Army. Power for the vehicle was provided by a 330hp engine that was supposed to be able to propel it at a maximum speed of 72mph. *(DOD)*

A line-up of the original model of the Category 1 MaxxPro MRAP in Afghanistan before going on patrol. On the roof of the vehicle is the open-topped Objective Gunners Protection Kit (O-GPK) also seen on the US Army M1114 and M1151 UAHs. Reflecting the threat posed by improvised explosive devices, the vehicle is fitted with a number of counter-IED devices. *(DOD)*

This 6 × 6 MRAP pictured is the original model of the Category 1 vehicle named the 'Caiman'. It was based on the chassis of the American military's 5-ton Family of Medium Tactical Vehicles (FMTV). It is powered by a 275hp engine that provides it a maximum speed of 55mph. The Caiman was 25 feet 7 inches in length, had a width 10 feet 1 inch and a height of 11 feet 9 inches. *(DOD)*

(*Opposite above*) As the enemy in both Iraq and Afghanistan developed ever larger and more powerful IEDs, the American military responded by fitting their MRAPs with ever more armour protection. Reflecting this, there appeared an up-armoured model of the 6 × 6 Caiman, seen here on a trailer, that was labelled as the Caiman-Tactical Vehicle System (TVS). It was quickly nicknamed the 'Caiman Plus'. (*DOD*)

(*Opposite below*) A 4 × 4 MRAP developed by Force Protection Inc that became known as the 'Cougar'. With the rush to deploy MRAPs such as the Cougar as quickly as possible, many were airlifted to Iraq. Obviously it would have been more affordable to ship them by sea. Some suggested that the need to ship them by air was the result of poor planning and a failure to adopt these vehicles for troop-use much earlier. (*DOD*)

(*Above*) A number of USMC 4 × 4 Cougar MRAPs preparing for a mission. The vehicle in the foreground is fitted with the open-topped Objective Gunners Protection Kit (O-GPK). The two vehicles in the background are fitted with the Marine Corps Transparent Armored Gun Shield (MCTAGS). The various versions of the 4 × 4 Cougar were 23 feet 2 inches in length, 9 feet wide and 8 feet 7 inches high. (*DOD*)

(*Opposite above*) Besides the various 4 × 4 versions of the Cougar there was a 6 × 6 model as seen here, which came in slightly different versions. The clear relationship between the 4 × 4 Cougar and the 6 × 6 Cougar is seen in the configuration of the front engine compartment, especially the hood design. Both the 4 × 4 and 6 × 6 versions of the Cougar series were also employed by British Army units in Iraq. (*DOD*)

(*Above*) This 6 × 6 example of the Cougar series of vehicles is fitted with a device known as the Vehicle Optics Sensor System (VOSS), designed and built by the Lockheed Martin Corporation. The ball-like sensor on the rear of the vehicle, seen in its stored position, is gyro-stabilized and contains a daylight optical camera, thermal-imaging camera and laser rangefinder. (*DOD*)

(*Opposite below*) Pictured on arrival in Kuwait is a 4 × 4 MRAP labelled as the RG-31. It was originally developed by a South African firm for their military, but was adopted by the American military and license-built by General Dynamics Land Systems (GDLS) in the United States. Incorporating lessons learned in combat, the RG-31 went through various upgrade programs that resulted in the RG-31A1 through to the RG-31A3. (*DOD*)

(*Above*) Positive results with the 4 × 4 RG-31 series led to the development and fielding of this larger 4 × 4 model that was referred to as the RG-33. Powered by a 400hp engine, it had a maximum speed on roads of 68mph. It is 28 feet in length, 8 feet in width and 9 feet 5 inches tall. As with all MRAPs, it is top heavy because of the need to have a certain amount of space between the bottom of its hull and an under-vehicle explosion. (*DOD*)

(*Opposite above*) Shown in Iraq is a Buffalo Mine Removal Vehicle that actually entered US Army service before the advent of the MRAP program, but was absorbed into that program when started. Except for the personal weapons of the crew, the vehicle was not armed. Its most noticeable external feature, besides its enormous size, is the fully articulated camera-equipped arm seen here in its stored position. (*DOD*)

(*Opposite below*) In the foreground is the base model of the MRAP All-Terrain Vehicle (M-ATV) and in the background the MaxxPro-Dash. The M-ATV had an independent suspension system, and combined with being smaller and lighter than all the other MRAPs proved more adept at patrolling the often steep and narrow roads encountered in Afghanistan. The M-ATV shown is fitted with the FRAG 7 armoured turret that comes with overhead protection for the gunner. (*DOD*)

(*Opposite above*) Despite being smaller than all the other MRAPs, the MRAP All-Terrain Vehicle (M-ATV) is still a fairly massive vehicle based on the size of the crew members seen alongside their vehicle. It has a length of 20 feet 6 inches, a width of 8 feet 2 inches and a height of 8 feet 7 inches. The vehicle can drive up a 60 percent slope and has both traction control and anti-lock brakes. (*DOD*)

(*Opposite below*) During the early days of the Iraq Insurgency, a group of US Army civilian workers in Kuwait decided to see if they could help the troops. They took a surplus armoured hull of an M113 APC and welded it to the chassis of a 5-ton truck. This had first been done during the Vietnam War but was eventually rejected by the US Army as being too time-consuming to construct in the numbers required. (*Randy Talbot*)

(*Above*) Preserved at a museum is this example of a small number of armoured gun trucks that were built and placed into service in Iraq prior to the advent of the MRAPs. The vehicle chosen for the conversion process was the standard 5-ton truck fitted with an armoured cab and cargo compartment. In the armoured cargo compartment were machine guns protected by transparent armoured panels. (*Brent Sauer*)

Notes

Notes

Notes

Notes

Notes

Notes

Notes